I0100758

Basics of Textile Chemical Processing

The Authors

Dr. Gopalakrishnan is presently working as an Assistant Professor in the Department of Costume Design & Fashion, SMS College of Arts and Science, Coimbatore. He has 7 years teaching and 7 years industrial experience. He has published more than 65 articles in journals of repute. He has published two books and presented more than 20 research papers in conferences.

Dr. T. Karthik is presently working as an Assistant Professor (Senior Grade) in the Department of Textile Te chnology, PSG College of Technology Peelamedu, Coimbatore. He has 5 years teaching, 5 years industrial and 5 years experience of handling various spinning subjects.

He has contributed more than 40 articles in International and National Journals of repute. He has published two books and contributed one book chapter. He is the member in Professional bodies such as TAI and MIE.

Basics of Textile Chemical Processing

Authors

D. Gopalakrishnan
Dr. T. Karthik

2016

Daya Publishing House®

A Division of

Astral International Pvt. Ltd.

New Delhi – 110 002

© 2016 AUTHORS

Publisher's note:

Every possible effort has been made to ensure that the information contained in this book is accurate at the time of going to press, and the publisher and author cannot accept responsibility for any errors or omissions, however caused. No responsibility for loss or damage occasioned to any person acting, or refraining from action, as a result of the material in this publication can be accepted by the editor, the publisher or the author. The Publisher is not associated with any product or vendor mentioned in the book. The contents of this work are intended to further general scientific research, understanding and discussion only. Readers should consult with a specialist where appropriate.

Every effort has been made to trace the owners of copyright material used in this book, if any. The author and the publisher will be grateful for any omission brought to their notice for acknowledgement in the future editions of the book.

All Rights reserved under International Copyright Conventions. No part of this publication may be reproduced, stored in a retrieval system, or transmitted in any form or by any means, electronic, mechanical, photocopying, recording or otherwise without the prior written consent of the publisher and the copyright owner.

Cataloging in Publication Data--DK
  Courtesy: D.K. Agencies (P) Ltd. <docinfo@dkagencies.com>

  Gopalakrishnan, D., author.
  Basics of textile chemical processing / authors, D. Gopalakrishnan, Dr. T. Karthik.
    pages cm
    Includes index.

  ISBN 978-93-5130-878-2 (International Edition)

  1. Textile chemistry.   I. Karthik, T., author. II. Title.

  TP893.G67 2016 DDC 677.02835   23

Published by   :   **Daya Publishing House®**
                              A Division of
                              Astral International Pvt. Ltd.
                              – ISO 9001:2008 Certified Company –
                              4760-61/23, Ansari Road, Darya Ganj
                              New Delhi-110 002
                              Ph. 011-43549197, 23278134
                              E-mail: info@astralint.com
                              Website: www.astralint.com

Laser Typesetting   :   **Classic Computer Services,** Delhi - 110 035

Printed at   :   **Thomson Press India Limited**

Preface

The textiles and clothing industry occupies a very important place in the Indian economy in terms of its share in employment, value added and export earnings. The Indian Textiles Industry has an overwhelming presence in the economic life of the country. Textiles have undergone wet chemical processing since time immemorial. Human ingenuity and imagination, craftsmanship and resourcefulness are evident in textile products throughout the ages; we are to this day awed by beauty and sophistication of textiles sometimes found in archeological excavations. Wet processing of textiles constitutes innumerable steps leading to finished product, each having a number of complex variables and every lot is like a new lot and much depends on the well-trained manpower rather than modern machines and technology.

The key to success in textile wet processing technology will be the indication of highly trained manpower at lucrative wages in structured manner. However, developments are taking place at a rapid pace to satisfy the user with quality product and competitive price. Though underlying principle for developments is satisfying user needs. This in turn will impart cost competitiveness. Globalisation is the buzz world today. One of the consequences of globalisation is competitiveness. That means consistent production of products at competitive prices. Textile processing occupies a predominant position in the entire textile value chain.

This book is intended to provide useful information to employers, management personnel, professionals, technocrats, supervisors and employees engaged in textile chemical processing. Though there are numerous books available in market related to textile wet processing, which are deeply chemistry oriented. So there is a need for simple understanding of concept for students and also for the basic level of people working in an industry. As every workplace has its own uniqueness, employers should develop their own programmes that best suit their workplaces with due consideration for the processes being carried out, the chemicals used, the working environment, the levels of training and experience of their employees. The field of textile processing as a profession is growing, and it is in the hope of furthering the dignity of this province of science that the authors present this volume to those whose work is related to this branch of the subject, whether in the scientific, the technical aspect. It is hoped, will be of assistance to both the practical operator in textiles and the student of textile subjects.

The introductory chapter contains an overview of pretreatment process and techniques, followed by an overview of the pretreatment processes individually. It also covers the function and application of various chemicals and auxiliaries used in textile processing. The environmental issues related to the textile wet processing have been addressed briefly.

D. Gopalakrishnan
Dr. T. Karthik

Contents

Preface   *v*

1. **Introduction**   1

   Pretreatment Processes and Techniques — Manufacturing Processes — Singeing — Desizing — Scouring — Mercerizing — Bleaching — Dyeing — Printing

2. **Singeing**   5

   Objectives and Advantages — Types of Singeing Machines — Plate Singeing Machine — Rotary-cylinder Singeing Machine — Gas Singeing Machine — Burning Behaviour of Cotton and Polyester — Important GAS Singeing Parameters — Flame Intensity — Fabric Speed — Distance between Flame Burner and Fabric — Flame Width — Essential Conditions for Good GAS Singeing — Important Considerations during GAS Singeing — Testing Singeing Effectiveness — Common Problems in Gas Singeing and their Causes — Incomplete Singeing — Uneven Singeing Across the Fabric Width — Uneven Singeing Along the Fabric Length

3. **Desizing**   13

   Sizing — Sizing Agents Based on Native Polysaccharides — Factors Influencing Desizing — Techniques for Removal of Starch-Based Sizes — Techniques for the Removal of Water Soluble Sizes — Techniques for the Removal of Water Soluble and Insoluble Sizes

4. **Mercerization**   19
    *At which Stage Cellulose can be Mercerized? — Chain Mercerizing Machine —
    Chainless Cloth Mercerising Ranges — Machine Features — Important Aspects of
    the Chainless System — Ammonia Mercerizing of Cellulose Fibres - Liquid
    Ammonia Mercersing Process — Causticizing (Alkali Treatment)*

5. **Bleaching**   29
    *Bleaching with Hydrogen Peroxide — Bleaching with Sodium Hypochlorite —
    Bleaching with Sodium Chlorite — Bleaching with Peracetic Acid*

6. **Dyes and Pigments**   35
    *Acid Dyes — Basic (Cationic) Dyes — Chemical Characteristics and General
    Application Conditions — Environmental Issues — Direct (Substantive) Dyes —
    Chemical Characteristics and General Application Conditions — Environmental
    Issues — Disperse dyes — Chemical Characteristics and General Application
    Conditions — Environmental Issues — Metal-complex Dyes — Chemical
    Characteristics and General Application Conditions — Environmental Issue —
    Mordant Dyes (Chrome Dyes) — Chemical Characteristics and General Application
    Conditions — Environmental Issues — Naphthol Dyes (Azoic Dyes Developed on
    the Fibre) — Chemical Characteristics and General Application Conditions —
    Application of Azoic Colourants Involves a Number of Steps — Environmental
    Issues — Reactive Dyes — Chemical Characteristics — Environmental Issues —
    Sulphur Dyes — Chemical Characteristics and General Application Conditions —
    Environmental Issues — Vat Dyes — Chemical Characteristics and General
    Application Conditions — Environmental Issues*

7. **Dyeing: Machinery and Techniques**   57
    *Loose Fibre - Autoclave — Yarn — Hank Dyeing Machines — Package Dyeing
    Machines — Fabric in Rope Form — Batch Processes — Jet Dyeing Machine —
    Overflow — Soft-flow — Continuous Processes — Airflow*

8. **Printing**   67
    *Printing Process Steps — Printing with Pigments — Printing with Dyes —
    Printing Paste Preparation — Printing (Paste Application) — Fixation — After-
    treatment — Ancillary Operations — Printing Technology — Flat-Screen Printing
    — Rotary-screen Printing — Roller Printing — Jet Printing*

9. **Traditional and Conventional Prints**   79
    *Kalamkari — Techniques of Kalamkari — Application of Myrobelums —
    Preparation of Black Colour Solution — Block Printing — Washing — Developing
    — Application of Yellow Colour — Growth of Dress out of Painting, Cutting —
    Significance of Madhubani Wall Painting — Colour Used for Painting — Brush
    Used for Painting — Material Used for Painting — Symbols Used in Madhubani
    Painting — Tie and Dye — Style of Dyed and Printed Textile of India — Tools and
    Accessories Required — Suitable Fabrics for Tie and Dye — Preparation of Materials*

*— Techniques of Tie and Dye — Dye Preparations and Methods of Dyeing —
Naphthol Dyes — Method of Preparation — After Treatment — Vat Dyes —
Method of Preparation — Dye Calculation — Precautions — Opening the Thread
of Tied Portion — Batik — Fabrics, Materials and Tools — Wax — Brushes —
Tjanting and Tjap — Tracing the Design on the Fabric — Application of Wax on
the Cloth — Dyeing Procedure — Removal of Wax from the Fabric — Methods of
Printing — Block Printing — Materials for Printing — Rapid Colours — Method
— After Treatments — Screen Printing — Stencil Printing — Design Suitable for
Stencil Printing — Tools and Materials — Procedure — Preparation of Stencil
Sheets — Air Brush or Gun Spray — Precautions — Roller Printing — Discharge
Printing — Bandhani — Patola — Patola or Ikkat Fabrics*

10. Finishing   **97**

*Antimicrobial Finishes — Odour Fights Finish — Anti-Static Finish — UV-
Protection — Flame Retardant Finish — Wrinkle Resistance — Nano Particles in
Finishing — Nano-Care — Key Features — Nano-Pel — Key Features — Nano-
Dry — Key Features — Nano-Touch — Key Features*

Index   ***103***

1

Introduction

Pretreatment Processes and Techniques

Pretreatment processes should ensure the removal of foreign materials from the fibres in order to improve their uniformity, hydrophilic characteristics and affinity for dyestuffs and finishing treatments. The improvement of the ability to absorb dyes uniformly (which is the case in mercerizing). The relaxation of tensions in synthetic fibres (without this relaxation of tension, unevenness and dimension instabilities can occur). The position of pretreatment within the production scheme is closely related to the position of dyeing in the sequence. The point is that pretreatment comes immediately before dyeing (and printing).

Pretreatment processes and techniques depend:

☆ On the kind of fibre to be treated: For raw goods made of natural fibres such as cotton, wool, flax and silk the technical task is more difficult than for those made of synthetic and artificial fibres. Natural fibres in fact are accompanied by a higher amount of substances that can interfere with later processing. Man-made fibres, in turn, usually contain only preparation agents, water-soluble synthetic size and soil.

☆ On the form of the fibre (flock, yarn, woven or knitted fabrics).

☆ On the amount of material to be treated (for example, continuous methods are more efficient, but are economically viable only for large production capacities).

☆ Pretreatment operations are often carried out in the same type of equipment used for dyeing (in batch processing, in particular, the material is most often pretreated in the same machine in which it is subsequently dyed).

Manufacturing Processes

Cotton pretreatment includes various wet operations, namely:

☆ Singeing

☆ Desizing

☆ Scouring

☆ Mercerizing

☆ Bleaching

Some of these treatments are obligatory steps only for certain make-ups (*e.g.* desizing is carried out only on woven fabric). Moreover some of these treatments are often combined together in one single step in order to respond to the need to reduce production time and space as much as possible.

Singeing

Singeing can be carried out both on yarns and woven fabrics, but it is more common on fabrics, especially on cotton, cotton/PES and cotton/PA substrates. Protruding fibre ends at the fabric surface disturb the surface appearance and produce an effect known as "frosting" when dyed. It is therefore necessary to remove the surface fibres by passing the fabric through a gas flame. The fabric is passed over a row of gas flames and then immediately into a quench bath to extinguish the sparks and cool the fabric. The quench bath often contains a desizing solution, in which case the final step in singeing becomes a combined singeing and desizing operation. Before singeing, the fabric is combed under aspiration to eliminate remaining dust and fibres. Singeing has no effect on the effluents because only cooling water is necessary. During singeing relatively strong odours and emissions of dust and organic compounds are observed. Odorous substances can be destroyed using catalytic oxidation techniques.

Desizing

Desizing is used for removing from woven fabric sizing compounds previously applied to warp and is usually the first wet finishing operation performed on woven fabric. Desizing techniques are different depending on the kind of sizing agent to be removed. Currently applied techniques can be categorized as follows:

1. Techniques for the removal of starch-based sizing agents (water-insoluble sizes).

2. Techniques for the removal of water-soluble sizes.

3. Techniques for the removal of water soluble and insoluble sizes.

Scouring

Scouring (also known as boiling-off or kier boiling) is aimed at the extraction of impurities present on the raw fibre or picked up at a later stage such as:

☆ Pectin

☆ Fat and waxes

☆ Proteins

☆ Inorganic substances, such as alkali metal salts, calcium and magnesium phosphates, aluminum and iron oxides

☆ Sizes (when scouring is carried out on woven fabric before desizing)

☆ Residual sizes and sizing degradation products (when scouring is carried out on woven fabric after desizing).

Scouring can be carried out as a separate step of the process or in combination with other treatments (usually bleaching or desizing) on all kind of substrates: woven fabric (sized or desized), knitted fabric and yarn. For yarn and knitted fabric, scouring is usually a batch process which is carried out in the same equipment that will subsequently be used for dyeing (mainly autoclaves or hank dyeing machines for yarn and overflows, jets, etc. for knitted fabric). Woven fabric is scoured in continuous mode using the pad-steam process.

Mercerizing

Mercerizing is carried out in order to improve tensile strength, dimensional stability and luster of cotton. Moreover an improvement in dye uptake is obtained (a reduction of 30 - 50 per cent of dyestuff consumption can be achieved, thanks to the increased level of exhaustion). Mercerizing can be carried out on yarn in hanks, woven and knitted fabric through one of the following different treatments:

☆ Mercerizing with tension

☆ Caustification (without tension)

☆ Ammonia mercerizing

Bleaching

After scouring, cotton becomes more hydrophilic. However, the original colour stays unchanged due to coloured matter that cannot be completely removed by washing and alkaline extraction. When the material has to be dyed in dark colours it can be directly dyed without need of bleaching. On the contrary, bleaching is an obligatory step when the fibre has to be dyed in pastel colours or when it will need to be subsequently printed. In some cases, even with dark colours a pre-bleaching step may be needed, but this is not a full bleaching treatment. Bleaching can be performed on all kinds of make-ups (yarn, woven and knitted fabric).

Common bleaching reagents include hydrogen peroxide, sodium hypochlorite, sodium chlorite, and Sulphur. The degree of bio-elimination should be >80 percent after 7 days. Hydrogen peroxide is the most commonly used bleaching agent for cotton and is typically used with alkali solutions. The use of chlorine-based bleaches may produce organic halogens (due to secondary reactions) and cause significant concentrations of Adsorbable organic halogens (AOX), particularly dichloromethane, in the wastewater. Sodium hypochlorite bleaching represents the most significant concern, and lower AOX formation should result if sodium chlorite bleaching is used. The wastewater is alkaline.

The most frequently used for Cellulosic fibres are oxidative bleaches, namely:

☆ Hydrogen peroxide (H_2O_2)

☆ Sodium hypochlorite (NaClO)

☆ Sodium chlorite ($NaClO_2$)

Apart from these, per acetic acid is also applicable. Also optical brightening agents are commonly used to obtain a whitening effect.

Dyeing

Various types of machines are used for processing fibres in loose form. These include conical pan machines, pear-shaped machines and radial flow machines. Yarn can be processed either in hank form or in package. Different machines are used depending on the method chosen. They are used for all wet operations, that is, pretreatment, dyeing, application of finishing agents and washing. Hank dyeing machines, Package Dyeing Machines are used for yarn dyeing commonly. The fabric should be processed by continuous and batch processes. Textile dyes can be classified according to their chemical composition (azo, antrachinone, sulphur, triphenil methane, indigoid, phthalocyanine, etc.) or according to their application class. At the industrial level the second method is preferred.

Printing

In the textile processing industry the printing section is the main process for fabric processing. Styles of printing as follows:

1. Direct style

2. Discharge style

3. Resist style

2

Singeing

Singeing can be carried out both on yarns and woven fabrics, but it is more common on fabrics, especially on cotton, Polyester/Cotton blends. Protruding fibre ends at the fabric surface disturb the surface appearance and produce an effect known as "frosting" when dyed. It is therefore necessary to remove the surface fibres by passing the fabric through a flame. Before singeing, the fabric is combed under aspiration to eliminate remaining dust and fibres. Singeing has no effect on the effluents because only cooling water is necessary. During singeing relatively strong odours and emissions of dust and organic compounds are observed. Textiles materials are most commonly singed in woven or knitted fabric form or in yarn form. Technically, singeing refers to the burning-off of:

☆ Loose fibres not firmly bound into the yarn and/or fabric structure;

☆ Loose yarns not firmly bound into the fabric structure;

☆ Protruding fibre ends sticking out of the textile yarns and/or fabrics.

Objectives and Advantages

☆ Singeing of a fabric is done in order to obtain a clean fabric surface which allows the structure of the fabric to be clearly seen.

☆ Fabrics, which have been singed, soil less easily than un-singed fabrics.

☆ The risk of pilling, especially with synthetics and their blends, is reduced in case of singed fabrics.

☆ Singed fabrics allow printing of fine intricate patterns with high clarity and detail.

☆ Singed fabric dyed in dark shades is considerably reduced, as randomly protruding fibres are removed in singeing which could cause diffused reflection of light.

Types of Singeing Machines

There are three main types of singeing machines:

1. Plate singeing machine
2. Rotary cylinder singeing machine
3. Gas singeing machine

Plate Singeing Machine

In this type of singeing machine, the cloth passes over and in contact with one or two heated curved copper plates. The thickness of the plates ranges from 1 to 2 inches. The heating of the plates is done by a suitable burning arrangement of gas mixed with air. The plates are heated to bright redness and the cloth passes over and in contact with these plates at a speed ranging from 150 to 250 yards per minute. The passage of the cloth can be arranged in such a manner that one or both sides of the fabric may pass over and in contact with the heated plate(s), in order to accomplish singeing of one or both sides of the fabric in a single passage. In order to avoid local cooling of a certain part of the plate(s) by constant passage of cloth over it, an automatic traversing mechanism is fitted to the machine. This mechanism brings the cloth into contact with a constantly changing part of the plate(s), not only to avoid local cooling but also local wearing of the plate(s).

Rotary Cylinder Singeing Machine

The material passage in the rotary cylinder singeing machine is shown in Figure 2.1. In this type of singeing machine, the cloth passes over and in contact with a heated rotary cylinder made of copper or cast iron. The rotary cylinder has internal firing and revolves slowly so that constantly a fresh surface of the roller comes in contact with the cloth. The direction of rotation of the cylinder is opposite to the direction of the fabric so that the protruding fibres or nap of the fabric is raised. This

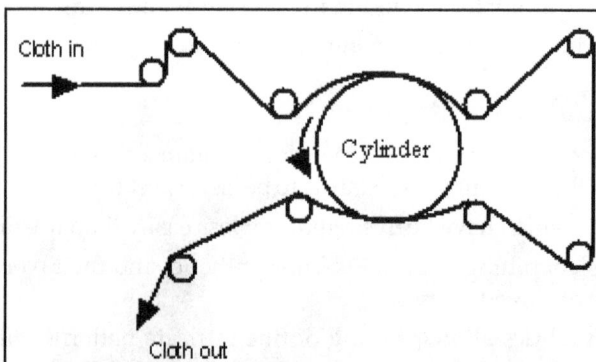

Figure 2.1: Rotary Cylinder Singeing Machine.

type of machine is particularly suitable for the singeing of velvets and other pile fabrics. If the singeing of both sides of the fabric is required, then two cylinders are employed, one for each side of the fabric.

Gas Singeing Machine

The material passage in the rotary cylinder singeing machine is shown in Figure 2.2. In this type of singeing machine, the fabric passes over a burning gas flame at such a speed that only the protruding fibres burn and the main body of the fabric is not damaged by the flame. This is the most common type of machine used for singeing fabrics as well yarns.

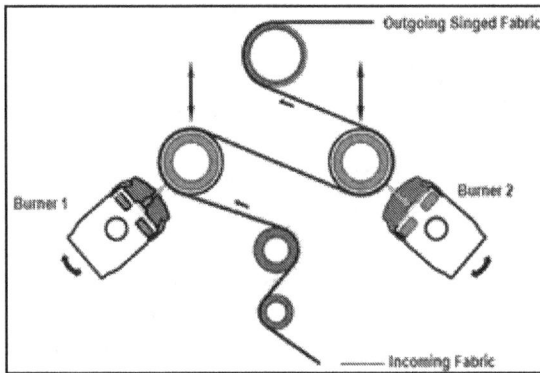

Figure 2.2: Gas Singeing Machine.

Fundamentals of Gas Singeing

The main purpose of singeing is to burn the protruding fibres from the yarn and/or fabric surface. In order to burn the protruding fibres, energy must be supplied. The supplied energy must be just enough to burn only the protruding fibres, while keeping the firmly bound fibres in tact. This is achieved by allowing time of contact between the singeing flame and the fabric to practically a fraction of a second. As the temperature of the flame is too high (around 1300°C), any regulation of this temperature is out of the question. However, metering and control of thermal energy of the flame is essential for the safe but effective burning off process.

Burning Behaviour of Cotton and Polyester

Cotton has an exothermic pyrolysis as once it has been ignited it continues to burn by virtue of its own energy which is being released. Polyester has an endothermic pyrolysis as it requires a steady supply of energy to allow the burning process to continue. Polyester ignites at a temperature of 480-500°C, while it starts melting at 250-260°C. For the singeing of polyester fabric or yarns, thermal energy must be supplied in a shock form, and the pyrolysis must be like an explosion, so that the polyester protruding fibres ignite rather than melting. Otherwise, molten beads of polyester may be formed. Pyrolysis refers to transformation of a substance by the action of heat. At temperature of pyrolysis (Tp), both thermoplastic and non-thermoplastic fibres decompose (pyrolyze) into lower molecular weight fragments.

The chemical change, which begins at temperature of pyrolysis, continues through the temperature of combustion (Tc).

At the start, the fabric passes through a tension unit with guide rollers and bars, which ensure crease-free entry of the fabric into the machine. Then, there are (optional) pre-drying cylinders which even out any variations in the fabric moisture-content and temperature. Next, the fabric passes through pre-brushing unit which, in addition to removing dirt/dust, lint and loose fibres from the fabric, causes the fibres sticking to the fabric surface to stand out for easy subsequent burning. A dust collection system, provided just below the brush rollers, is connected to a powerful suction unit. After pre-brushing, the fabric enters into the singeing chamber, where it passes over the burning flames, which are positioned on both sides of the fabric. The cloth can be threaded so as to allow singeing of either one or both sides of the fabric. Burner body is specially designed to provide gas flow at uniform pressure/velocity throughout the fabric width. Burner is termed as the heart of singeing and should generate homogenous, stable, uniform and highly concentrated flame rich in energy by ideal combustion of the gas and air mixture. Good singeing machines offer adjustable flame intensity, flame width and distance between the flame and the fabric.

Gas outlet section of the burner is provided with water jacket to keep the burner cool. Adjustable water-cooled rollers are used to obtain different fabric/flame positions, which permit desired degree of singeing effect on different quality of fabrics by adjusting the guide roller position with respect to the flame. A Carburetor or air/gas mixer allows automatic mixing of gas with air to control the intensity of the singeing flame. After passing over the flames, the fabric passes through (optional) steam quenching unit to put off any sparks and/or through post-brushing section for clean-up/removal of burnt fibres. The after-brushing keeps the subsequent impregnation-liquor cleaner and reduces the amount of dust entering in the following process steps. Then, the fabric passes though a saturator, which contains the desizing agent along with the auxiliary chemicals. After saturation with the desizing liquor, the fabric is squeezed by squeezing mangles and is wound on a batcher.

Important GAS Singeing Parameters

1. Flame intensity
2. Fabric speed
3. Singeing position
4. Distance between flame burner and fabric
5. Flame Width.

Flame Intensity

Together with the supply and control units for gas-air mixture, burners comprise the most important part of any singeing machine. The flame intensity of the singeing burners is based on the amount and the outlet speed of the gas-air mixture leaving the burner slots. Besides having high thermal energy, flame also has considerable mechanical energy. All the thermal and mechanical energy of the flame is directed onto the fabric during singeing. The temperature of the flame at the mouth of the burner is in the range of 1250 to 1300°C. The speed of the flame at the burner outlet may be between 15 and 35 metre per second. The flame intensity usually lies between 5 and 20 mbars.

Fabric Speed

The fabric speed in the singeing machine is usually in the range of 50-160 m/min depending on fabric (gram per square metre) weight and fibre blend. For heavier fabrics, the speed is kept slower as compared to lighter weight fabrics.

Distance between Flame Burner and Fabric

As the energy content of the flame is lower the farther it is from the burner, the singeing efficiency is consequently decreased by increasing the burner-fabric distance. The distance between the burner and the fabric is usually in the range of 6-8 mm but it can be adjusted in a range from 6-20 mm.

Flame Width

All good singeing machines come with a provision of flame width adjustment according to the width of the fabric. This is essential to optimize the gas economy.

Essential Conditions for Good GAS Singeing

Following are three essential conditions for good singeing:

1. A flame with high mechanical and thermal energy to quickly burn thermoplastic protruding fibres (*e.g.* polyester) without any molten beads formation.

2. A homogeneous flame with uniform mechanical and thermal energy to result in uniform singeing.

3. An optimal flame/fabric contact time to neither results in incomplete not over-singeing.

Important Considerations during GAS Singeing

☆ Make sure that the flame is more bluish (less yellowish) to give the maximum temperature.

☆ Control and maintain the recommended flame length and angle of contact, depending on the fabric construction, thickness, weight, heat sensitivity, etc.

☆ Regulate the fabric speed according to the fabric construction/thickness/weight etc.

☆ Make sure that all the burner nozzles are free from choking. Choking of nozzles may result in the appearance of haziness, patchy appearance or faint lines, which become apparent after dyeing.

☆ Make sure that the machine is threaded through the machine correctly. Rubbing marks may show up if the fabric is threaded wrongly over defective stationery bars and/or if the fabric rubs against the burners. (As the guide rollers are very close to the burners, any problems due to loose brackets supporting the rollers will guide the fabric to touch the burner block/nozzle). Invariably such defects only show up after dyeing or finishing, at which stage it is difficult to attribute the cause to the singeing machine operation.

☆ Make sure that the threading is as per specification drawing so that both sides of the fabric are singed. Singeing on only one side of the fabric may result in face to back shade variation after dyeing.

☆ Make sure that the width of the flame is set to cover just a little more than the fabric width. This will ensure conservation of energy.

☆ Make sure that the exhaust blowers over the burners are in proper operation. If not, it can lead to re-deposition of the burnt out fibres on the fabric causing black specks.

☆ Ensure appropriate quenching into water/desize bath after singeing. Otherwise, the entrapped smoldering particles may lead to fabric getting burnt (holes).

☆ Guide rolls next to the flames or the guide rollers on which flame is directed in case of heat-sensitive fabrics should be cooled, generally by cold water circulating through the guide rollers. Otherwise they could become red hot and scorch the fabric.

☆ Interlinking of stop button/flame switch-off mechanism/quenching system should be effective to avoid burning of the fabric and any incident of fire.

Testing Singeing Effectiveness

The effectiveness of singeing process can be checked by one or more of the following:

☆ By looking at the singed fabric with magnifying glass and comparing its hairiness with that of the un-singed fabric. A well-singed fabric shows less hairiness.

☆ By testing the singed fabric for pilling performance and comparing it with that of the un-singed fabric. A well-singed fabric gives less pilling.

☆ By sticking and removing a sticking tape on the singed fabric and observing the number of fibres attached to the sticking side of the tape. A well-singed fabric results in less number of fibres sticking on the tape.

☆ Noticing the feel or handle of the singed fabric. An over-singed fabric may give a harsher feeling.

Common Problems in Gas Singeing and their Causes

Incomplete Singeing

1. The most common causes of incomplete singeing are as follows:
2. Too low flame intensity
3. Too fast fabric speed
4. Too far distance between the fabric and the burner

5. Inappropriate (*i.e.* less severe) singeing position
6. Too much moisture in the fabric incoming for singeing.
7. If the fabric incoming for singeing has too much moisture in it, a significant amount of thermal energy will be used up in evaporating the fabric moisture rather than burning the protruding fibres, resulting in incomplete singeing.

Uneven Singeing Across the Fabric Width

The most common causes of width ways uneven singeing are as follows:

1. Non-uniform moisture content across the fabric width
2. Non-uniform flame intensity (uneven flame height) across the fabric width
3. Uneven distance between the burner and the fabric, this may be due to misalignment or improper setting of the guide rollers
4. Uneven smoke evacuation over the burners

Uneven Singeing Along the Fabric Length

1. The most common causes of lengthways uneven singeing are as follows:
2. Non-uniform moisture content along the fabric length
3. Non-uniform flame intensity along the fabric length, variation in gas-air mixture supply, Increasing or decreasing thermal energy of the flames during production
4. Change in fabric speed during singeing
5. Change in the distance between the fabric and the burner along the length.

3

Desizing

Desizing is used for removing from woven fabric sizing compounds previously applied to warp and is usually the first wet finishing operation performed on woven fabric.

Desizing techniques are different depending on the kind of sizing agent to be removed. Currently applied techniques can be categorized as follows:

☆ Techniques for the removal of starch-based sizing agents (water-insoluble sizes)

☆ Techniques for the removal of water-soluble sizes

☆ Techniques for the removal of water soluble and insoluble sizes.

Sizing

In order to lubricate and protect the warp yarn during weaving, sizing agents (in the form of water solutions or water dispersions) are applied after warping. The main sizing agents can be grouped into two classes:

Sizing Agents Based on Native Polysaccharides

☆ Starch

☆ Starch derivates such as carboximethyl starch or hydroxyl ethyl starch ether

☆ Cellulose derivates, especially carboximethyl cellulose (CMC)

☆ Galactomannans

☆ Protein derivates.

Fully Synthetic Polymers

☆ Polyvinyl alcohols (PVA)

☆ Polyacrylates

☆ Polyvinyl acetate

☆ Polyester

The ratio of synthetic sizing agents to native sizing agents is variable (*e.g.* about 1:3 in Germany, 1:4 - 1:5 in Spain).

Factors Influencing Desizing

☆ The type of sizing agent applied varies according to the fibres to be processed, the weaving technique adopted and the demands of any system used for recycling the sizing agents

☆ Sizing agent formulations are usually mixtures of the substances mentioned above.

☆ With cotton, additional auxiliaries are present in the sizing mixtures.

These are mainly:

☆ **Viscosity regulators**: Complex formation between borax and the hydroxyl groups of starch increases the viscosity of the paste, while urea reduces it. Important viscosity regulators include starch-degrading agents such as peroxo disulphates, peroxo sulphates that act by oxidative cleavage of the macromolecules

☆ **Sizing fats:** Used to improve the weaving behaviour of the warp. Suitable materials include sulphated fats and oils and mixtures of fatty acid esters with non-ionic and anionic emulsifiers (mainly based on polyglycol ethers).

☆ **Wetting agents:** Fatty alcohols poly (glycol ethers) with a low degree of ethoxylation.

☆ **De-foaming agents:** Their addition is often necessary when the sizing agents tend to produce foam (*e.g.* with PVA) or if wetting agents are added. Suitable products are based on paraffin oils, phosphoric esters, fatty acid esters or silicone oils.

☆ **Preservatives:** for sizing liquors that are stored for long periods and contain degradable components such as starch and starch derivatives, fungicides and/or bactericides are added. Typical preservatives include formaldehyde, phenol derivatives, and heterocyclic compounds of the isothiazoline type.

Sizing agents used for synthetic fibres (*e.g.* polyacrylates, polyesters) do not contain these auxiliaries, except for the preservatives, which are always to prevent bacteria attack present when aqueous systems are used.

Sizing agents are introduced by the weaving firm, but have to be removed by the finisher (during the operation called desizing). This desizing process results in high waste water loads. In the case of woven fabric, sizing agents can represent 30 - 70 per cent of the total COD load in waste water. The lower percentage is for finishing of woven fabric mainly consisting of flat filament yarns and the higher for staple fibres, especially for cotton and in case of native sizing agents. Therefore it is important to know the COD of these substances and their characteristics in terms of biodegradability and bio-eliminability. Note that additives present in the formulations (*e.g.* the preservatives) also influence the aquatic toxicity and biodegradability of the resulting emissions (toxicity and biodegradability cannot be discriminated by using only COD measurements).

Techniques for Removal of Starch-Based Sizes

Starch-based sizes are difficult to remove and require either catalytic action of an enzyme (catalytic degradation) or other chemical treatment in order to be converted into a washable form. This chemical degradation is mainly achieved by either enzymatic or oxidative desizing. *Enzymatic desizing* is the most widely used method for the removal of starch, amylases being particularly suitable. The advantage in the use of enzymes is that starches are decomposed without damaging cellulose fibre.

In order to reduce the number of steps in the pretreatment process, it is common practice to combine desizing with cold bleaching in a single step. In this case the process is also called *"oxidative desizing"*. The fabric is impregnated in a bath containing hydrogen peroxide and caustic soda, together with hydrogen peroxide stabilizers and complexing agents. Persulphate is also usually added to the solution. Due to the action of NaOH, this treatment, beside a desizing/bleaching effect, also serves as a pre-scouring treatment. Furthermore, oxidative desizing is particularly useful when the textile contains enzyme poisons (fungicides) or when sizes are present that are difficult to degrade. Desizing is usually carried out in pad-batch, but discontinuous (*e.g.* Jigger Figure 3.1) and continuous (pad-steam) processes can also be applied. In the case of enzymatic desizing, pad-steam is applied only for big lots and with enzymes that are stable under steaming conditions. After the reaction time, the fabric is thoroughly washed in hot water (95 °C). Enzymatic desizing using amylases is an established process that has been in use for many years. More recently, pectinases have shown promise in replacing the traditional alkaline scouring treatment. Some auxiliary suppliers have introduced an enzymatic process to remove hydrophobic and other non-cellulosic components from cotton. The new process operates at mild pH conditions over a broad temperature range and can be applied using equipment such as jet machines. The environmental benefits remain unclear as enzymes contribute to the organic load and their action is based on hydrolysis rather than oxidation. The organic load not removed with enzymatic desizing may appear in the later wet processing steps. A more global balance would probably reveal no significant improvement.

Techniques for the Removal of Water Soluble Sizes

The removal of water-soluble sizes such as PVA, CMC and polyacrylates, theoretically only requires washing with hot water and sodium carbonate. However, the washing efficiency can be increased by:

☆ Adding suitable auxiliaries (wetting agents) to the desizing liquor (with some restrictions in case of size recovery)

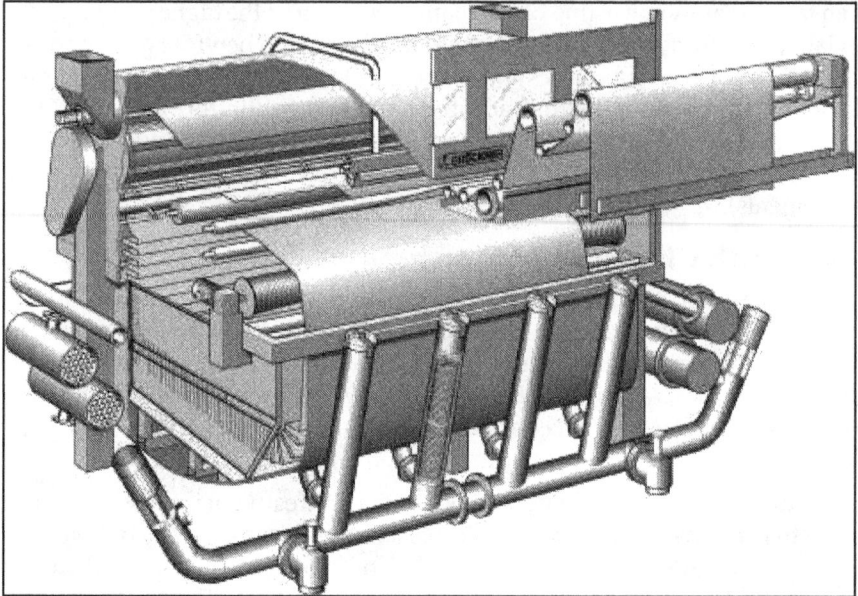

1 Window
2 Fabric
3 Take up roll
4 Let-off roll
5 Liquor
6 Guiding devices

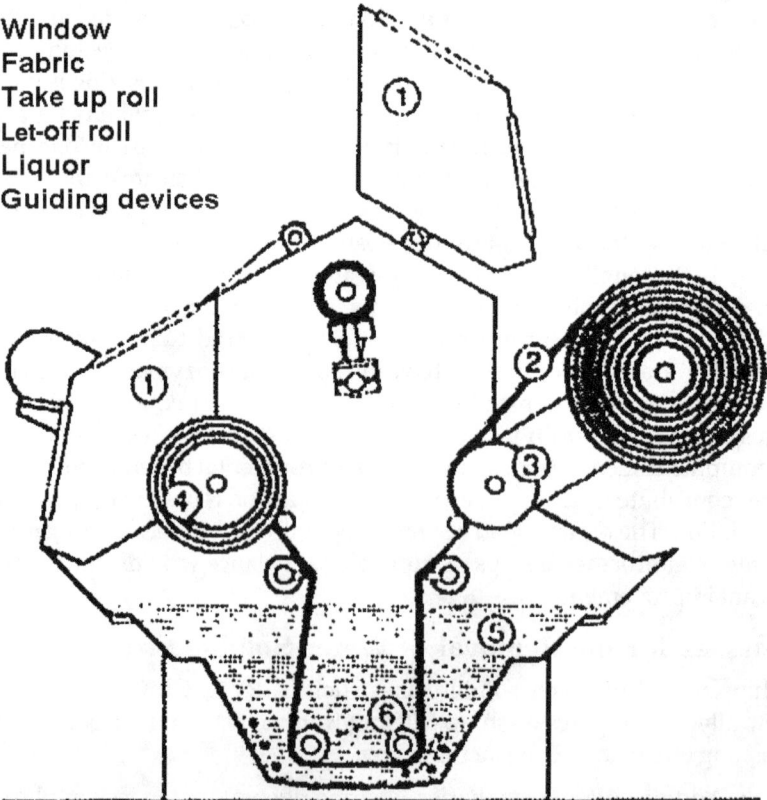

Figure 3.1: Schematic Representation of a Jigger.

☆ Allowing adequate time for immersion in the desizing liquor (this ensures maximum liquor pick-up and adequate time for the size to swell).

☆ Washing thoroughly with hot water in order to remove the solubilised size.

In this case the process is carried out in normal washing machines. Continuous washers are often used, but sometimes the treatment time may be too short to allow complete desizing. Pad-batch and pad-steam or discontinuous processes for prolonging the residence time are therefore also in use.

Techniques for the Removal of Water Soluble and Insoluble Sizes

The oxidative desizing technique mentioned above is applicable not only for water insoluble sizing agents, but also for water soluble ones. This technique is particularly useful for textile finishers dealing with many different types of fabrics and therefore sizing agents.

4

Mercerization

Mercerization is one of the most important processes of finishing cotton materials. It imports gloss to the fibre, increases its hygroscopicity, strength and improves its dye affinity. The mercerizing process consists in treatment of Cellulosic materials with concentrated solutions of caustic soda at a temperature of 15 to 18°C. Mercerized cellulose is hydrated cellulose, *i.e.*, a product which from the chemical point of view is identical to the original cellulose, but differing from it in physical properties. This method was patented in 1850 by the English calico printer John Mercer and hence this process has been called as mercerization. Under the action of concentrated alkaline solutions chemical, physico-chemical and structural modifications of cellulose take place. Chemical reactions lead to the formations of alkali cellulose, physical reactions, to intensive swelling of fibres and structural reactions, to a change in the arrangement of units in the cellulose macromolecule. When the fibre swells, its volume undergoes considerable changes; at maximum water absorption, the cross section of cotton fibre is increased by 40 to 50 per cent with inconsiderable increase in length (about 1 to 2 per cent). The size of pores in the fibrous material is considerably increased.

The main factors influencing the factors of swelling are temperature of treatment, the concentration of the alkali in the solution and additions made to the solution. Cellulose swelling in an alkaline solution increases with a drop of temperature. Alkali concentration is also of great importance for the cellulose swelling. The greatest swelling of cotton cellulose is observed at alkali concentrations characterized by an appearance of an X-ray pattern of alkali cellulose.

At which Stage Cellulose can be Mercerized?

☆ On greige goods

☆ After desizing

    After desizing and scouring

    After bleaching

☆ After dyeing.

Woven fabrics are mercerized in full width, knitted fabrics in full width or in rope form. The sodium hydroxide concentration varies from 20 per cent - 30 per cent. The process, done in a continuous way, consists of the following steps:

☆ Padding of the textile with the lye

☆ Drafting of the textile

☆ Washing (under tension)

☆ Acidifying, rinsing.

Chain Mercerizing Machine

The material passage in a chain mercerizing machine is shown in Figure 4.1. In this machine the mercerising lye causes fabric shrinkage, it is necessary to arrange the machine compliments in such a manner that the finished fabric satisfies the dimensional requirements in all respects.

A. Fabric entrance section: The fabric is taken of from its plighted condition through a set of automatic cloth guiders, guide rollers and tension bars.

B. Impregnation section: In the case of the chain type mercerising machines, impregnation with the mercerising lye is carried out in suitably dimensioned padding mangles. The mercerising lye having an optimum concentration of caustic soda is continuously fed to the trough of the padding mangle. The single web of fabric gets a dip in the lye and is then passed through the padding mangle, where the excess lye is squeezed out from the impregnated cloth. Small machines have one padder. Whenever more mercerising production is required, the passage through one padder is not sufficient to make up the lye action time. A second impregnation is, therefore introduced in the system. Usually, two lye pads give the required production, but, for still higher production speeds, a third impregnation padder is necessary. It is necessary to decide on the expected production before the installation of the mercerising range.

C. Width stretching and stabilizing section: The reduction in width of the fabric due to shrinkage is to be recovered by stretching the impregnated cloth in at the stenter. Weak lye is sprayed on the fabric, while it is being stretched in the stenter frame.

D. Steam recuperation zone: After squeezing the fabric at the end of the stenter through the squeezing mangle, the fabric is introduced into the lye recuperation section, where steam heated water, near boil, in the

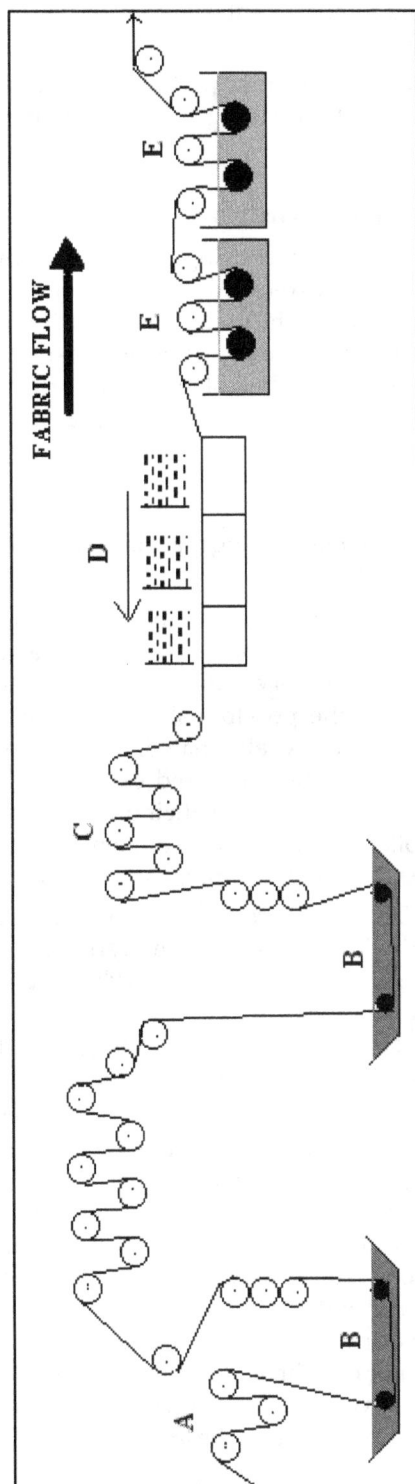

Figure 4.1: Chain Mercerizing Machine.

A: Fabric entrance section; B: Impregnation section; C: Width stretching and stabilizing section; D: Steam recuperation zone; E: The washing section.

recuperation washing compartment with top and bottom rollers, recovers the major quantity of lye.

E. **The washing section:** The remaining portion of the lye is washed out of the cloth in the washing section having the requisite number of washing compartments.

Chainless Cloth Mercerising Ranges

The material passage in a chain mercerizing machine is shown in Figure 4.2. The chainless mercerising machines are so-called, because there is no fabric stretching by clip-chains in this type of machines. The underlying principle in these machines is to apply tension to the fabric before and during the mercerising process and not to allow the cloth to shrink, till it reaches their stage when shrinking does not take place, with a view to achieve satisfactory mercerising results with reasonable production speeds.

Machine Features

The features of chainless cloth mercerising machines can be briefly mentioned as follows:

A. **Fabric entrance:** This consists of the entrance scaffolding, automatic cloth guiders, tension bars and a fabric pre-tensioning system. These parts take care of their ceaseless cloth passage to the mercerising section with sufficient the tensioning, so that the possible shrinkage during the action of mercerising lye can be almost eliminated. The pre-tensioning system consists of three curved rubber covered expanding rollers, in which necessary tension can be developed by their proportional displacement of the middle curved roller. At the end of the pre-tensioning section, the fabric is introduced into the mercerising impregnating compartment.

B. **Lye impregnation:** The lye impregnation section consists of cylindrical metal rollers, partially immersed in the mercerising alkali lye, having a specific gravity of 56° TW. Rubber covered cylindrical metal rollers rest above and between the metal rollers. These rollers cease their good impregnation and restrict the weft wise shrinkage and they also provide the means of fabric traction through the machine. There is an arrangement to spray the lye over the fabric in the impregnation compartment.

C. **Adjustable squeezing devices:** At the end of each section of the chainless mercerising machine, provision is made for an effective adjustable squeezing device. In the case of longer impregnating compartments, it becomes necessary to arrange for an additional squeezing device within the impregnation section. This is necessary in order to complete the lye impregnation at that pre-determined speed and to cope up with the production target. The driven rollers of the squeezing devices are connected to the D. C. multi motor coordinated driving system. One of the drives is arranged as the pilot drive and all the preceding and succeeding drives are co-ordinated in such a manner that the tension in the Warp and the Weft

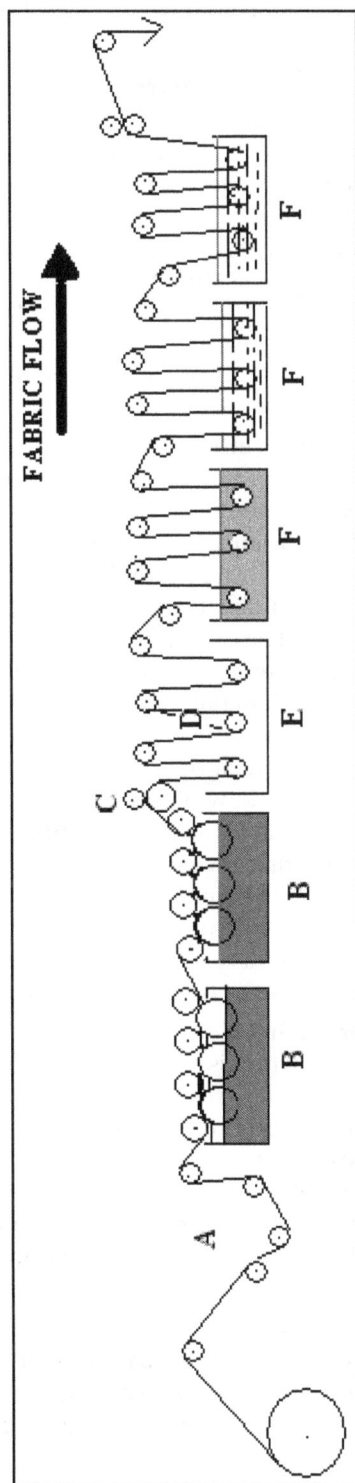

Figure 4.2: Chainless Pad less Mercerizing Machine.

A: Fabric entrance; B: Lye impregnation (Caustic solution); C: Adjustable squeezing devices; D: Adequate number of top and bottom rollers; E: Recuperation of the mercerizing lye; F: Washing Zones.

directions is maintained which is very essential for achieving a good degree of mercerization.

D. **Adequate number of top and bottom rollers:** With a view to obtain a perfect mercerising effect, it is necessary that the cloth should be in contact with the lye for the predetermined lye acting time. It can be understood that the more the number of rollers, the longer the dwelling time. The idea is that the lye acting time of 50 seconds can be arranged by designing the impregnation compartment to suit the ideal level, by adjusting the number of rollers in the impregnation compartment as correctly as possible. In some chainless mercerising machines, there may be an additional set of metal and rubber covered rollers, which help in covering up the lye acting time. For higher dwell times, the machine speed to be reduced. Similarly for Shorter lye acting time, the speed is to be increased.

E. **Stabilization of the mercerising effect:** As has been explained earlier, there will be uncontrollable shrinkage in the fabric, if the mercerising lye contents are very quickly reduced from the mercerising cloth. In order not to allow this shrinkage to take place, the initial treatment of the cloth should be with a weak lye solution. The stabilizing action is obtained in the stabilizing section. In some cases, the stabilization is brought about by passing the mercerized fabric over a set of an expanding system consisting of three or more rows of metallic segmented curved revolving rollers. This expanding system is also called my cock stretching contrivance. This stretching device exercises a widthwise stretching effect, thus giving a much better width control over the lye impregnated fabric. The entire arrangement including the weak lye spray-over the fabric, while on my cock rollers, is termed "the stabilizing section". The strength of the weak lye sprayed is generally about half the strength of the mercerising lye strength. The weak lye can be stored separately and is sprayed on the fabric in the section in the form of the a good spray, by means of their circulation pump and is spraying system. This possible shrinkage from this stage of the fabric to the fully washed stage is not appreciably and can be controlled without much difficulty.

F. **Recuperation of the mercerising lye:** The mercerising lye picked up by the cloth during the process and which is still on the fabric after the stabilization is required to be recovered, *i.e.*, recuperated, to a great extent in the recuperation section. This section comprises a tank, with top and bottom rollers. The fabric passes over the top and bottom rollers, during which passage it is treated with hot water, maintained at the temperature of 90° Celsius are slightly above. Heating of the water and maintaining the temperature are carried out by means of a closed steam coil.

G. **Neutralizing the lye on the cloth:** After coming out of the recuperation, the mercerized and hot water washed fabric is passed through a squeezing device into the neutralizing section. This section is provided with an arrangement to wash the fabric with a weak acid solution. Neutralizing with an acid solution is necessary only when there is no further alkali boiling process or any other wet process which requires the use of alkali containing solutions. Whenever mercerising is carried out before bleaching, neutralizing is not required. This section is provided with a device to introduce a predetermined acid dose automatically. Whenever as in addition is not to be carried out, the neutralizing compartment can be used as a normal washing compartment.

H. **Washing Zone:** The purpose of the washing zone, which may consists of one, two or more washing compartments, is to wash the mercerising fabric free from alkalinity. As explained above, whenever a further boiling process is called for, the presence of small traces of residual alkali may not be objectionable. However, if there is any overnight stoppage of the washing process, a thorough wash is recommended to avoid any staining part other takes of defects in the mercerized cloth.

I. **Tension regulation system:** The chainless mercerising machines are characterized by their continuous fabric can, with free selvedges. this means that there is no direct stretch exerted on the fabric width. The fabric run, therefore, needs a constant consistent control and a thorough regulation of the fabric tension, that is, fabric width. Inadequate tension in the lye impregnating section would mean a corresponding loss in the cloth width, which is a very adverse factor, as for us the user is concerned. the tension in the cloth to be maintained is, usually, in the ascending order in mercerising, *i.e.*, cloth entry, cloth impregnation, lye action, and stabilization section. On the other hand, once the mercerising action is completed, the cloth tension should be in the descending order, that these recuperating, neutralizing and the washing zones.

J. **Versatility of the chainless mercerising machines by way of the choice of fabric webs:** The chainless mercerising machines give the processor the choice of the number of fabric webs to be processed, which will be based on the narrowness of the cloth width as also on the fabric weight per square metre. Such novel variations are possible only in the chainless system, because the cloth salvages are not to be gripped in the chain clips and are free. It is also necessary to remember that the fabric is not allowed to run on its own, but is constantly held between rollers till the mercerising process is completed and only washing the lye a way remains to be carried out.

Important Aspects of the Chainless System

The following points are very important and should be borne in mind in respect of the chainless mercerising machines:

1. Good lye pickup but not in excess of the mercerising needs, that it, say, 1 kg of mercerising lye per 1 kg of fabric.

2. Good length of continuous lye impregnation gives a better degree of mercerization.

3. Excellent squeezing effect at the pneumatic squeezing devices, regulating the lye pick up to the optimum level.

4. Wet fabrics (including gray material) can be processed, thus eliminating drying one process altogether (by pre-squeezing).

5. Closed circuit washing of the treated cloth gives good results with less quantity of wash water.

6. When all the safeguards and precautions are properly observed, the chainless mercerising machine offers an improved over all mercerising efficiency.

In order to achieve top quality mercerising results, the following optimum conditions are now being observed:

1. Strength of mercerising lye - 28° to 30° Bé.

2. Time of impregnation - 40 to 50 seconds

3. The lye temperature - 15° to 25°C

The polyester/cotton blends also give very good results under the above conditions. However, it is possible to obtain very satisfactory results with a slightly higher lye strengths and lower lye acting time, say, above 25 to 30 seconds. The main ecological impact in mercerising is the high concentrated residual lye.

Ammonia Mercerizing of Cellulose Fibres – Liquid Ammonia Mercersing Process

Stable shaping process technology opens the doors to fashion, a transitory fantasy determining the form, colour, design and new effects of textiles and clothing. This process, presently, is typical in fashionable cotton industry products and is also one of the mature technologies developed in textile and fibre industry. The features such as fitness, comfort, easiness to stretch, etc., are highly desired today. New purified cotton is a quality product material made using this high technology that overcomes the traditional flaws of shrinkage, wrinkled clothes, and improves dramatically the natural properties of softness, comfort of cotton. 'Liquid ammonia finishing or liquid ammonia mercerizing' refers to the process that truly revives the cotton through the expansion of liquid ammonia at an ultra-low temperature inside the fibre. When the cotton fibre is treated at -33°C liquid ammonia, ammonia at ultra low temperature will permeate immediately into the crystallographic structure of the fibre. Stress will be released through interior expansion, which makes the fibre cavity round and smooth, and rearranges the molecular structure, thus the crystallographic structure becomes slack and stable. This physical change makes the surface of the entire fabric smooth and bright, with solid and soft feel, so elasticity and wash-and-wear is fully achieved. The benefits of liquid ammonia mercerizing lies in the following effects that can be achieved simultaneously:

☆ Low shrinkage post washing.

☆ Increase in wrinkle resistance.

☆ Increase in fibre elasticity.

☆ Softer to touch and brighter.

☆ Enhanced tensile strength.

Causticizing (Alkali Treatment)

Similar effects to mercerising can be achieved by the Causticizing process. Causticizing in comparison to mercerising is done without tension stress on the textile at temperatures between 10°C and 15°C. The process induces shrinking of the textiles. Ecological impacts in Causticizing can be compared to mercerising.

5

Bleaching

After scouring, cotton becomes more hydrophilic. However, the original colour stays unchanged due to coloured matter that cannot be completely removed by washing and alkaline extraction. When the material has to be dyed in dark colours it can be directly dyed without need of bleaching. On the contrary, bleaching is an obligatory step when the fibre has to be dyed in pastel colours or when it will need to be subsequently printed. In some cases, even with dark colours a pre-bleaching step may be needed, but this is not a full bleaching treatment. Bleaching can be performed on all kinds of make-ups (yarn, woven and knitted fabric).

The most frequently used for Cellulosic fibres are oxidative bleaches, namely:

☆ Hydrogen peroxide (H_2O_2)

☆ Sodium hypochlorite (NaClO)

☆ Sodium chlorite ($NaClO_2$).

Apart from these, peracetic acid is also applicable. Also optical brightening agents are commonly used to obtain a whitening effect.

Bleaching with Hydrogen Peroxide

Bleaching can be carried out as a single treatment or in combination with other treatments (*e.g.* bleaching/scouring or bleaching/scouring/desizing can be carried out as single operations). The textile is treated in a solution containing hydrogen peroxide, caustic soda and hydrogen peroxide stabilizers at pH 10.5–12. The bleaching agent of peroxide is not the anion HOO⁻, but the dioxide radical anion OO˙⁻ (also known as superoxide). In competition with the formation of the bleaching agent, the OH* radical is formed, which is responsible for attacking and depolymerising the cellulose fibre. The formation of the OH* radical is catalyzed by metals such as iron, manganese and copper. The prevention of catalytic damage as a consequence of uncontrolled formation of OH* is mostly taken care of by using complex formers that inactivate the catalyst (stabilizers). Sodium silicate together with Mg salts ($MgCl_2$ or $MgSO_4$) and sequestering/complexing agents (EDTA, DTPA, NTA, gluconates, phosphonates and polyacrylates) are commonly used as stabilizers.

Other auxiliaries used in hydrogen peroxide bleaching are surfactants with emulsifying, dispersing and wetting properties. Employed surfactants are usually mixtures of anionic compounds (alkyl sulphonates and alkyl aryl sulphonates) with non-ionic compounds such as alkylphenol ethoxylates or the biologically degradable fatty alcohol ethoxylates.

Operating temperatures can vary over a wide range from ambient to high temperature. Nonetheless, a good bleaching action occurs when operating at around 60 - 90°C.

Bleaching with hydrogen peroxide in neutral conditions (pH range of 6.5 - 8) is also possible in some cases (*e.g.* when treating cotton in blends with alkali-sensitive fibres such as wool). At these pH conditions activators are required to give bleaching activity. Note that below pH 6.5, H_2O_2 decomposes into H_2O and O_2 by HOO^-/O_2^- disproportionation. Under these conditions hydrogen peroxide is wasted (production of inactive O_2 gas).

A wide range of bleaching processes can be used, including cold pad-batch, bleaching under steaming conditions and bleaching processes in long bath. Because the bleaching agent of peroxide is anionic in nature (hydrophilic behaviour), it is not possible with this bleaching method to destroy selectively the coloured hydrophobic material present on natural fibres without attacking the polymer itself.

Bleaching with Sodium Hypochlorite

The continuous bleaching with sodium hypochlorite is shown in Figure 5.1. The high reactivity of this bleaching agent imposes softer operative conditions than hydrogen peroxide (pH 9 - 11 and temperatures not above 30 °C). Otherwise there is a risk of damage to the cellulose fibre. The bleaching stage is followed by an anti-chlorine treatment in order to eliminate completely the hypochlorite and decompose the chloramines generated during bleaching. Bleaching with sodium hypochlorite can be carried out in batch (*e.g.* overflow, jet, jigger, and winch beck), semi-continuous (pad-batch) or continuous mode. A two-stage process is also in use in which hypochlorite and hydrogen peroxide are used. The use of hypochlorite as bleaching agent is in decline for ecological reasons. It is still applied for yarn and knitted fabric when a high degree of whiteness is required, for articles that remain white (*e.g.* linen), or require a white background or in processes where the ground-dye is discharged with a bleach treatment.

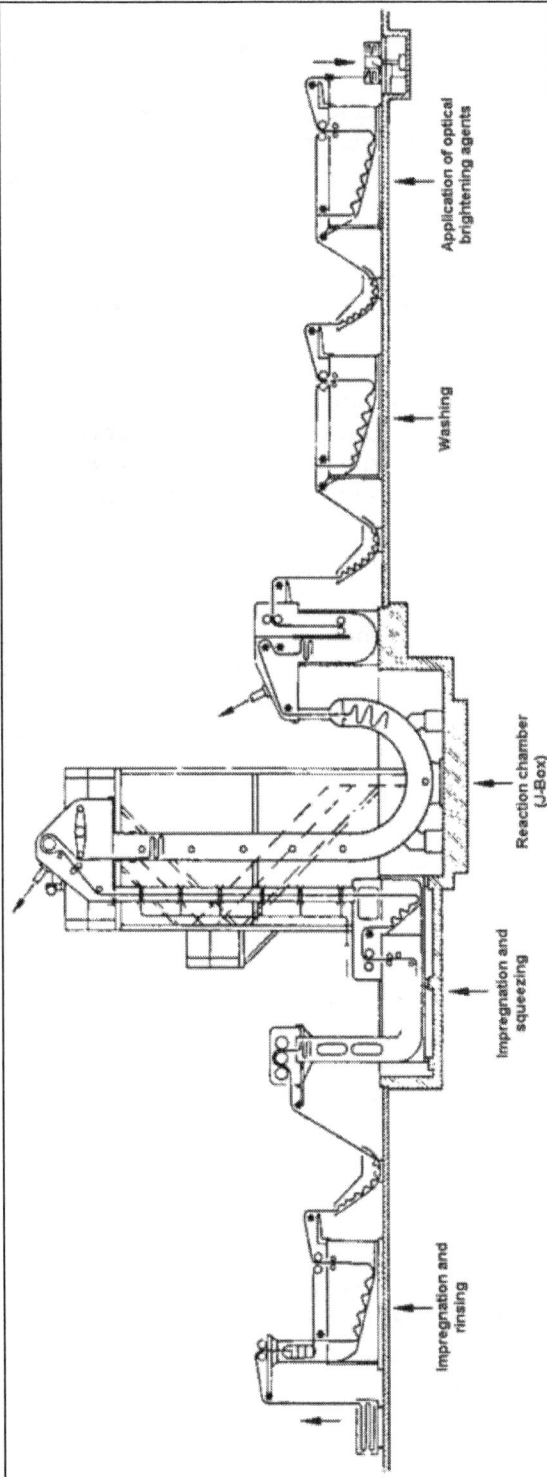

Figure 5.1: Continuous Bleaching with Sodium Hypochlorite.

Bleaching with Sodium Chlorite

Chlorite/chlorate bleaching, although in decline, is still applied for synthetic fibres, cotton, flax and other Cellulosic fibres, often in combination with hydrogen peroxide. The bleaching agent is the chlorine dioxide gas (ClO_2), which follows a completely different working mechanism compared to hydrogen peroxide. Whereas the super oxide radical ion in hydrogen peroxide is hydrophilic and therefore works preferentially in the hydrophilic region of the fibre (attack of the fibre polymer), ClO_2 absorbs preferentially on the hydrophobic associated material, such as the woody part of bast fibres. For this reason it is an excellent bleaching agent (ensuring a high degree of whiteness and no risk of damage of the fibre) especially for synthetic fibres and for bast fibres such as flax where, compared to cotton, there is a higher percentage of hydrophobic impurities. Because chlorine dioxide is unstable as a gas and can only be stored as a solution of approximately 1 per cent in water, it must be generated on-site as an aqueous solution. There are two ClO_2 precursor chemicals in present general industrial use, namely sodium chlorite and sodium chlorate. Although sodium chlorate is considerably less expensive than sodium chlorite, it is more difficult and expensive to convert to ClO_2, which explains why it is less commonly used. The continuous bleaching with sodium chlorite is shown in Figure 5.2.

Both sodium chlorite and sodium chlorate are used in strong acid conditions (pH 3.5 - 4 by formic or acetic acid). Chlorine dioxide solutions have a great corrosive action on construction materials including stainless steel. Sodium nitrate is used as a corrosion inhibitor to protect the stainless steel parts of equipment. It is also necessary to select detergent/wetting agents that can resist acid conditions. On the other hand, sequestering agents are not necessary because the oxalic acid used for acidification also serves for sequestering metals. The order of introduction of the different auxiliaries has to be controlled to avoid direct contact between the concentrated sodium chlorite/chlorate solution and acids. The textile material is bleached by padding or in long bath processes. The temperature is normally kept at 95°C, but cold procedures have also been developed to diminish toxicity and corrosion problems, using formaldehyde as an activator for sodium chlorite.

The advantages of chlorine dioxide bleaching are the high degree of whiteness and the fact that there is no risk of damage to the fibre. The main disadvantages are the high stresses to which the equipment is subjected and the chlorine residues that may be left on the fibre, depending on the way chlorite (or chlorate) is produced and activated. Recent technologies using hydrogen peroxide as the reducing agent of sodium chlorate are now available to produce ClO_2 without generation of AOX.

Bleaching with Peracetic Acid

Peracetic acid is produced from acetic acid and hydrogen peroxide. It can be purchased as ready-made product or produced in-situ. Its optimal bleaching action is reached only in a very narrow pH range between 7 and 8. Below pH 7 the degree of whiteness decreases sharply and above pH 9 depolymerization of the fibre with consequent damage of the fibre occurs.

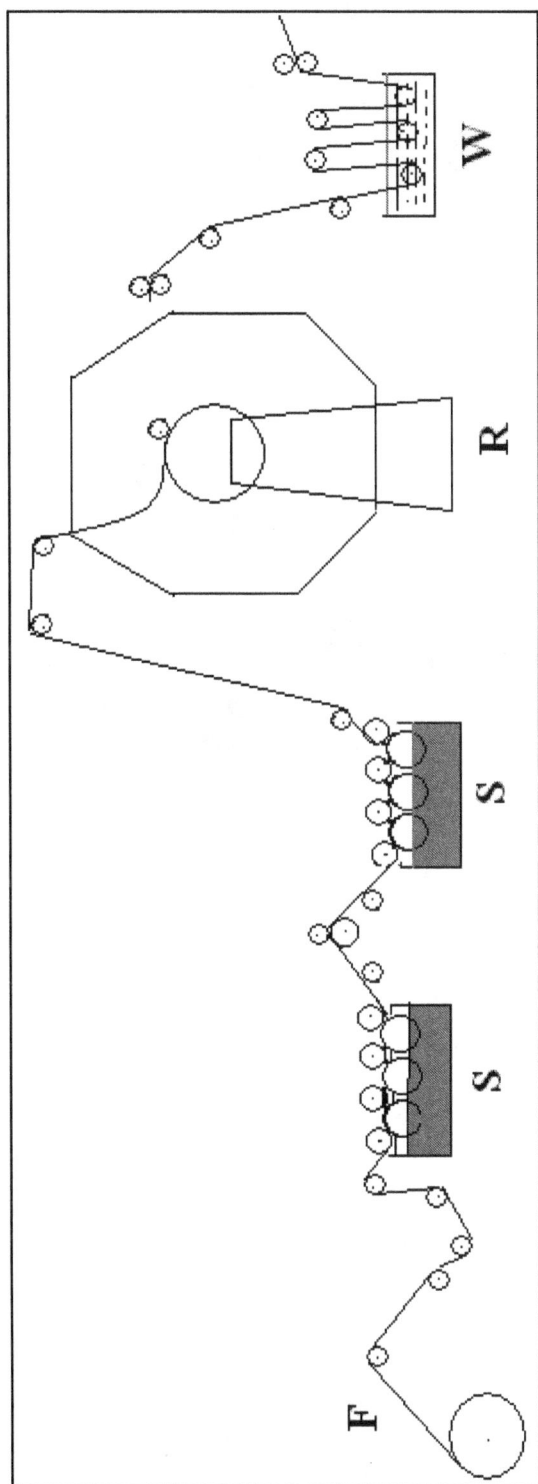

Figure 5.2: Continuous Bleaching with Sodium Chlorite.

6

Dyes and Pigments

Textile dyes can be classified according to their chemical composition (azo, antrachinone, sulphur, triphenil methane, indigoid, phthalocyanine, etc.) or according to their application class. At the industrial level the second method is preferred.

Acid Dyes

Acid dyes are mainly applied to polyamide (70 - 75 per cent) and wool (25 - 30 per cent). They are also used for silk and some modified acrylic fibres. Acid dyes exhibit little affinity for cellulose and polyester fibre. Colours are generally bright and fastness to light and washing range from poor to excellent, depending on the chemical structure of the dyestuff. Acid dyes are azo (the largest group), anthrax quinone, triphenil methane, Cu phthalocyanine chromophore systems which are made water-soluble by the introduction in the molecule of up to four sulphonate groups. The example of acid dyes are shown in Figure 6.1.

Their interaction with the fibre is based partly on ionic bonds between sulphonate anions and the ammonium groups of the fibre, as shown below for wool and for polyamide, at different pH conditions as shown in Figure 6.2.

Moreover, the fibre/dye interaction is based on secondary bonds such as Vander Waals forces. Secondary bonds are established in particular in the case of higher molecular weight dyes, which form aggregates with high affinity for the fibre. In use, acid dyes are classified by their dyeing behaviour and wet fastness properties, rather than chemical composition, hence the generic term acid dyes includes several individual dye classes.

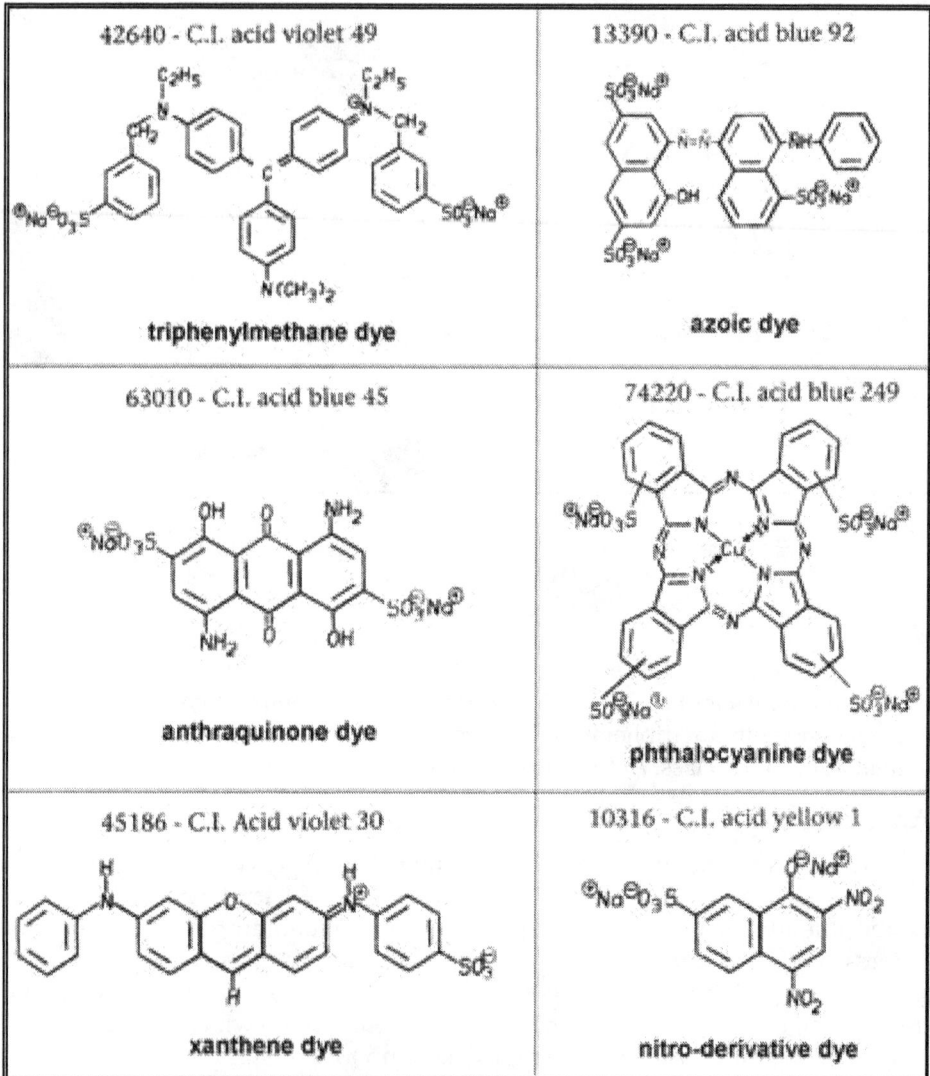

Figure 6.1: Examples of Acid Dyes.

The arbitrary classification normally adopted, in order of increasing fastness is:

☆ Level-dyeing or equalizing acid dyes

☆ Fast acid, half-milling or perspiration-fast dyes

☆ Acid milling dyes

☆ Super milling dyes.

Level-dyeing or equalizing dyes are subdivided into two classes, mono sulphonated (mainly for PA) and disulphonated (mainly for wool). Due to their poor

$$\overset{\oplus}{N}H_3 \quad \overset{\ominus}{O}_3S\text{-Col}$$

$$W$$

$$\text{COOH}$$

$$pH \simeq 5 \quad \text{Col-S}\overset{\ominus}{O}_3 \ \overset{\oplus}{H}_3\text{N-R-}.....\text{-}\bar{N}H\text{-CO-}.....\text{-R-COOH}$$

$$pH < 3 \quad \text{Col-S}\overset{\ominus}{O}_3 \ \overset{\oplus}{H}_3\text{N-R-}.....\text{-}\overset{\oplus}{N}H\text{-CO-}.....\text{-R-COOH}$$
$$\overset{\ominus}{O}_3\text{S-Col}$$

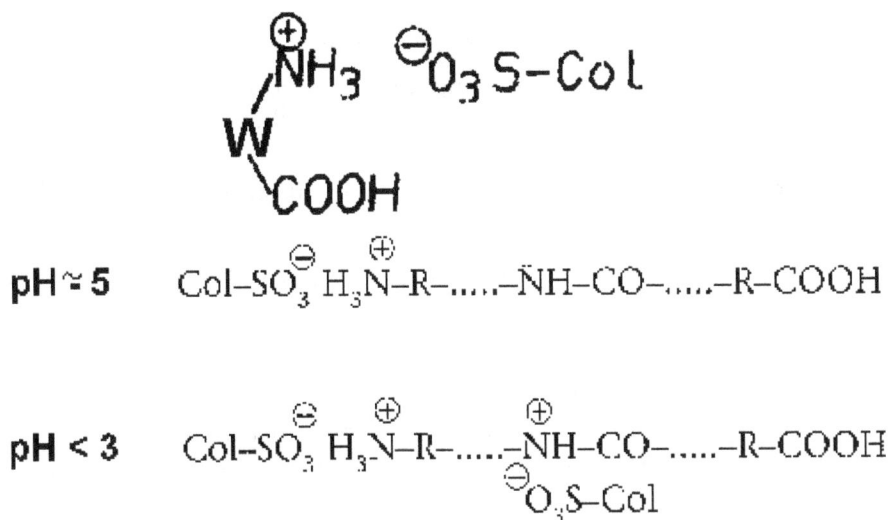

Figure 6.2: Interaction of Fibre and Dyes.

affinity for the fibre, they all have very good leveling properties. Their wet fastness is, however, sometimes poor, limiting their use to pale/medium shades.

Fast acid dyes (also known as half-milling dyes or perspiration-fast dyes) are only used for PA. They are generally mono sulphonated and exhibit superior fastness properties to level-dyeing acid dyes, while retaining some of the migration properties. The shade range available in this class is not as wide as that of the leveling or milling dyes and they therefore tend only to be used when alternatives would have poorer fastness properties.

Acid milling dyes are so named because they have a degree of fastness to the wet treatments employed when milling (mild felting) woolen fabrics. The class is further subdivided to include super-milling dyes, which have good wet fastness properties, arising from long alkyl side-chains attached to the chromophore. Due to their high molecular weight, milling dyes have a good affinity for the fibre and do not migrate well at the boil. Milling dyes are used mainly for wool for those applications where good wet fastness is required, for example in the dyeing of loose fibre which will receive a further wet treatment during hank scouring.

Depending on the class they belong to, acid dyes are applied under pH conditions that vary from strongly acidic to more neutral ones (3 - 7.5). For low-affinity dyes it is necessary to increase the level of cationization of the fibre (by acidification) in order to improve dye uptake. Conversely, dyes with higher molecular weight and high affinity would adsorb too rapidly on the fibre if applied under such strongly acidic conditions.

The most common chemicals and auxiliaries applied when dyeing with acid dyes are:

☆ Sodium sulphate (for level-dyeing and fast acid dyes), sodium acetate and ammonium sulphate (for acid milling dyes)

☆ pH regulators: acetic, formic and sulphuric acid, but also (typically for PA in the carpet sector) NaOH, NH_3 salts, phosphoric acid salts and higher (hydroxy) carboxylates

☆ Leveling agents, mainly cationic compounds such as ethoxylated fatty amines.

The most common chemicals and auxiliaries applied when printing with acid dyes are:

☆ Thickening agents

☆ Solubilising agents such as urea, thiourea, thiodiglycol, glycerine

☆ Acid donors: ammonium sulphate, tartrate or oxalate

☆ Defoamers (*e.g.* silicone oils, organic and inorganic esters) and «printing oils» (mainly mineral oils)

☆ After treatment agents such as formaldehyde condensates with aromatic sulphonic acids.

Basic (Cationic) Dyes

Basic dyes were initially used to dye silk and wool (using a mordant), but they exhibited poor fastness properties. Nowadays these dyestuffs are almost exclusively used on acrylic fibres, modified polyamide fibres, and blends. On acrylic fibres fastness performances are excellent.

Chemical Characteristics and General Application Conditions

Cationic dyes contain a quaternary amino group which can be an integral part (more common) or not of the conjugated system. Sometimes a positively-charged atom of oxygen or sulphur can be found instead of nitrogen. Ionic bonds are formed between the cation in the dye and the anionic site on the fibre. The examples of basic dyes are shown in Figure 6.3.

Cationic dyes are slightly soluble in water, while they show higher solubility in acetic acid, ethanol, ether and other organic solvents. In dyeing processes, they are applied in weak acid conditions. Basic dyes are strongly bound to the fibre and do not migrate easily. In order to achieve level dyeing, specific leveling auxiliaries, (also called retarders) are normally employed (unless a pH controlled absorption process is used). The most important group of retarders is represented by quaternary ammonium compounds with long alkyl side-chains (cationic retarders). Electrolytes and anionic condensation products between formaldehyde and naphthalene sulphonic acid may also be found.

Environmental Issues

The following dyestuffs have been classified as toxic by ETAD:

1. Basic Blue 3, 7, 81

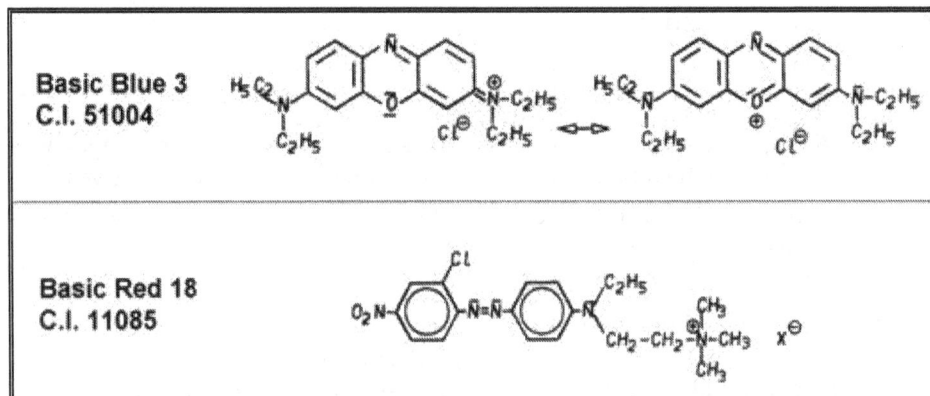

Figure 6.3: Examples of Typical Basic Dyes.

2. Basic Red 12
3. Basic Violet 16
4. Basic Yellow 21.

Direct (Substantive) Dyes

Direct dyes are used for dyeing cotton, rayon, linen, jute, silk and polyamide fibres. Colours are bright and deep, but light-fastness can vary greatly depending on the dyestuff. Wash fastness properties are also limited unless the textile is after-treated. Only occasionally are direct dyes used in direct printing processes.

Chemical Characteristics and General Application Conditions

Direct dyes (also called substantive dyes) can be azo compounds, stilbenes, oxazines, or phtalocyanines. They always contain solubilising groups (mainly sulphonic acid groups, but carboxylic and hydroxyl groups can also be found) that ionize in aqueous solution. Direct dyes are characterised by long planar molecular structures that allow these molecules to align with the flat cellulose macromolecules, the dye molecules being held in place mainly through Vander Waals forces and hydrogen bonds. Direct dyes may require the use of the following chemicals and auxiliaries for satisfactory dyeing:

☆ Electrolytes, usually sodium chloride or sodium sulphate. Their function is to favor the aggregation of dye ions on the fibre.

☆ Wetting and dispersing agents: mixtures of non-ionic and anionic surfactants are used for this aim.

☆ After treatment agents: they are used to improve wet-fastness properties. So-called fixative cationic agents are the most commonly used. They are usually quaternary ammonium compounds with long hydrocarbon chains. Formaldehyde condensation products with amines, poly nuclear aromatic phenols, cyanamide or dicyandiamide may also be used for this purpose.

Environmental Issues

   ✮ **Ecological properties of direct dyes**

   ✮ **Eco-toxicity:** Direct Orange 62 has been classified as toxic by ETAD.

   ✮ **Aromatic amines:** The main emphasis of research for direct dyes was actually on the replacement of possibly carcinogenic benzidine dyes.

   ✮ **Unfixed colourant:** Degree of fixation in batch dyeing processes ranges from 64 - 96 per cent.

Disperse dyes

Disperse dyes are used mainly for polyester, but also for cellulose (acetate and triacetate), polyamide and acrylic fibres. Fastness to light is generally quite good, while fastness to washing is highly dependent on the fibre. In particular, in polyamides and acrylics they are used mostly for pastel shades because in dark shades they have limited build-up properties and poor wash fastness.

Chemical Characteristics and General Application Conditions

Disperse dyes are characterized by the absence of solubilising groups and low molecular weight. From a chemical point of view more than 50 per cent of disperse dyes are simple azo compounds, about 25 per cent are anthraquinones and the rest are methine, nitro and naphthoquinone dyes.

The dye-fibre affinity is the result of different types of interactions:

   ✮ Hydrogen bonds

   ✮ Dipole-dipole interactions

   ✮ Vander Waals forces.

Disperse dyes have hydrogen atoms in their molecule, which are capable of forming hydrogen bonds with oxygen and nitrogen atoms on the fibre. Dipole-dipole interactions result from the asymmetrical structure of the dye molecules, which makes possible electrostatic interactions between dipoles on the dye molecules and polarized bonds on the fibre. Vander Waals forces take effect when the molecules of the fibre and colourant are aligned and close to each other. These forces are very important in polyester fibres because they can take effect between the aromatic groups of the fibre and those of the colourant.

Disperse dyes are supplied as powder and liquid products. Powder dyes contain 40 - 60 per cent of dispersing agents, while in liquid formulations the content of these substances is in the range of 10 - 30 per cent. Formaldehyde condensation products and lignin sulphonates are widely used for this purpose. Disperse dyes are widely used not only for dyeing, but also for printing synthetic fibres. Dyeing with disperse dyes may require the use of the following chemicals and auxiliaries:

   ✮ **Dispersants:** although all disperse dyes already have a high content of dispersants, they are further added to the dyeing liquor and in the final washing step.

☆ **Carriers:** For some fibres, dyeing with disperse dyes at temperatures below 100°C requires the use of carriers. This is the case with polyester, which needs the assistance of carriers to enable an even penetration of disperse dyes below boiling temperature. Because of environmental problems associated with the use of these substances, polyester is preferably dyed under pressure at temperature 100 °C without carriers. However, carrier dyeing is still important for polyester-wool blends, as wool must not be submitted to wet treatment at temperatures significantly above 100°C.

☆ **Thickeners:** Polyacrylates or alginates are usually added to the dye liquor in padding processes. Their function is to prevent migration of the dye liquor on the surface during drying.

☆ **Reducing agents (mainly sodium hydro sulphite):** They are added in solution with alkali in the final washing step.

Environmental Issues

☆ **Bio-eliminability:** Owing to their low water-solubility, they are largely eliminated by absorption on activated sludge in the waste water treatment plant

☆ **Organic halogens (AOX):** Some disperse dyes can contain organic halogens, but they are not expected to be found in the effluent after waste water treatment (because they are easily eliminated by absorption on the activated sludge)

☆ **Toxicology:** The following disperse dyes potentially have an allergenic effect: Disperse Red 1, 11, 17, 15; Disperse Blue 1, 3, 7, 26, 35, 102, 124; Disperse Orange 1, 3, 76; Disperse Yellow 1, 9, 39, 49, 54, 64.

☆ **Aromatic amines:** These dyes are still offered by some Far East dealers and manufacturers.

☆ **Unfixed colourants:** Level of fixation is in the range of 88 - 99 per cent for continuous dyeing and 91 - 99 per cent for printing.

☆ **Effluent contamination:** By additives in the dye formulation, Conventional dispersants (formaldehyde condensation compounds, lignin sulphonates, etc.) are poorly biodegradable (<30 per cent according to ca. 15 per cent according to some dyes are formulated with more readily eliminable dispersants (albeit not suitable for all formulations).

Metal-complex Dyes

Metal-complex dyes (also called pre-metalized dyes) have great affinity for protein fibres. Among metal-complex dyes, 1:2 metal-complex dyes are also suitable for polyamide fibres. More than 65 per cent of wool is today dyed with chrome dyes (see next section) or metal-complex dyes and about 30 per cent of PA is dyed with 1:2 metal-complex dyes. Light-fastness is excellent, while washing fastness is not as good as with chrome dyes (particularly in darker shades).

Chemical Characteristics and General Application Conditions

Metal-complex dyes may be broadly divided into two classes, 1:1 metal-complexes, in which one dye molecule is co-ordinated with one metal atom and 1:2 metal complexes, in which one metal atom is co-ordinated with two dye molecules. The dye molecule will be typically a mono-azo structure containing additional groups such as hydroxyl, carboxyl or amino groups, which are capable of forming strong co-ordination complexes with transition metal ions, typically chromium, cobalt, nickel and copper. Note that phthalocyanine dyes cannot be classified as metal-complex dyes. The examples of metal complex dyes are shown in Figures 6.4 and 6.5.

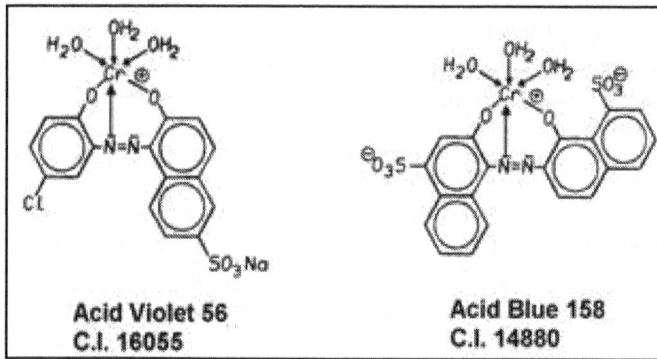

Acid Violet 56
C.I. 16055

Acid Blue 158
C.I. 14880

Figure 6.4: Examples of Metal-Complex Dyes.

Metal-complex dyes do not represent a specific application dye class. Metal-complex dyes belong in fact to many application classes of dyes (*i.e.* they can be found, for example, among acid, direct and reactive dyes). When used in dyeing processes, metal-complex dyes are applied in pH conditions regulated by the user class and the fibre type (wool, polyamide, etc.). The pH levels for wool range from strongly acidic (1.8 - 4 for 1:1 metal-complex dyes) to moderately acidic neutral (4 - 7 for 1:2 metal-complex

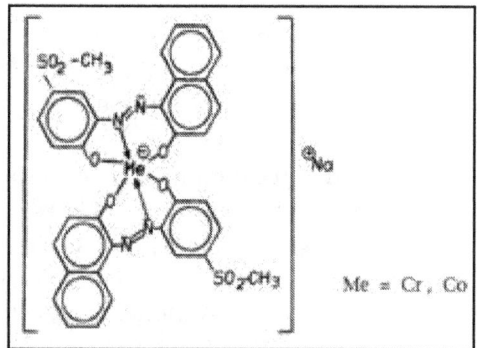

Figure 6.5: Examples of Metal-Complex Dyes.

dyes). For polyamide fibres higher pH conditions are becoming more and more common. 1:1 metal-complex dyes exhibit excellent level dyeing and penetration characteristics and have the ability to cover irregularities in the substrate. Their light and wet fastness properties are good even in deep shades. They are particularly suitable for yarn and for piece dyeing of carbonized wool.

1:2 metal-complex dyes are used for both wool and polyamide. They form the most important group in this class and may be divided into two sub-groups:

☆ **Weakly polar 1:2 complexes**: Solubilised by the inherent anionicity of the complex or containing non-ionic, hydrophilic substituent such as methyl sulphone ($-SO_2CH_3$). These dyes exhibit excellent fastness to light and wet treatments and excellent penetration properties.

☆ **Strongly polar 1:2 complexes:** Solubilised by one or more sulphonic or carboxylic acid residues, these dyes possess lower leveling power than the weakly polar dyes mentioned above but superior wet fastness properties and are generally suitable for use in those applications where mordant dyes are used. This second group is also more suitable for dyeing polyamide fibres.

Dyeing with metal-complex dyes may require the use of the following chemicals and auxiliaries:

☆ **pH regulators:** Sulphuric, formic, acetic acid

☆ **Electrolytes:** Sodium sulphate, ammonium acetate and sulphate

☆ **Levelling agents:** Mixtures of anionic and non-ionic surfactants (these auxiliaries are not needed when using pH controlled adsorption dyeing techniques).

Environmental Issue

☆ **Bio-eliminability:** Great differences from dye to dye (bio-eliminability can be <50 per cent)

☆ **Organic halogens (AOX):** Some products contain organic halogens: AOX in waste water therefore depends on the eliminability of the dyes concerned.

☆ **Heavy metals:** Metals can be found in the effluent due to unfixed dye. However, Cr III and the other transition metals used in metal-complex dyes are an integral part of the chromophore.

☆ **Unfixed colourants:** Degree of fixation ranges from moderate to excellent (from 85 to 98 per cent and greater in some cases).

☆ **Effluent contamination:** By additives in the dye formulation, Inorganic salts are present in the preparation of powder dyes. These salts, however, do not present any ecological or toxicological problems.

Mordant Dyes (Chrome Dyes)

Mordant dyestuffs are generally used for protein (wool and silk). They are practically no longer used for polyamide fibres or for printing. Good leveling properties and very good wet fastness after chroming, chrome dyes are used principally to obtain dark shades (greens, blues and blacks) at moderate cost. There are disadvantages, however, in their use: long dyeing times, difficulties with shading, the risk of chemical damage to the fibre during chroming and the potential release of chromium in waste water.

Chemical Characteristics and General Application Conditions

The Colour Index classifies these colourants' as mordant dyes, but chromium has become the almost universally used mordant and the class is commonly referred to as chrome dyes. From a chemical point of view they can be regarded as acid dyestuffs that contain suitable functional groups capable of forming metal complexes with chrome. They do not contain chrome in their molecule, which instead is added as dichromate, or chromate salt to allow dye fixation. Interaction with the fibre is established through ionic bonds formed between the anionic groups of the colourant and ammonium cations available on the fibre. In addition chromium acts as a link between dye and fibre. This gives rise to a very strong bond, which is reflected in the excellent fastness obtained. Figure 6.6 shows the ionic and coordination bonds in the case of wool.

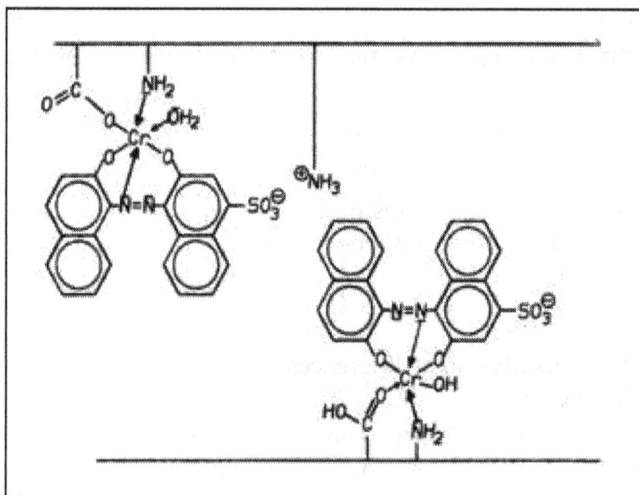

Figure 6.6: Ionic and Coordination Bonds between Wool and Chrome Dyes.

The use of chrome dyes in dyeing processes requires the use of the following chemicals and auxiliaries:

☆ Potassium and dichromate or chromate

☆ Formic or acetic acid as pH regulators

☆ Other organic acids such as tartaric and lactic acid. They are used to enhance the degree of conversion of Cr VI to Cr III

☆ Sodium or ammonium sulphate.

The typical coupling and developing agents for naphthol dyes are shown In Tables 6.1 respectively.

Environmental Issues

☆ **Heavy metals:** Chromium present in the final colourants is not contained in the molecule, being instead added as dichromate, or chromate salt during the dyeing process to allow dye fixation. The typical fast colour salts present in the colourants are shown in Figure 6.7.

Table 6.1: Typical Coupling Components for Naphthol Dyes

Colour Index		Formula
Diazo component n°	Chemical composition n°	
2	37005	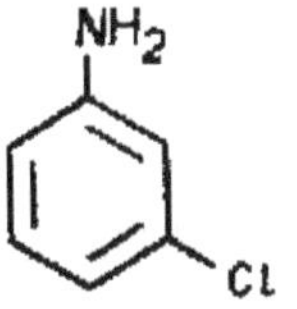
3	37010	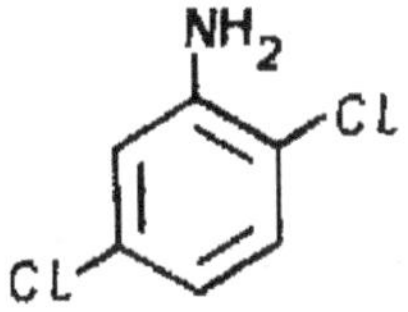
6	37025	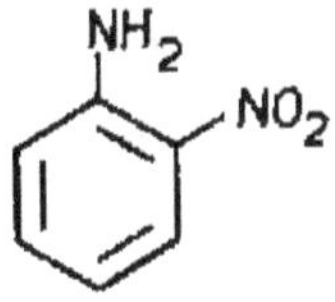
32	37090	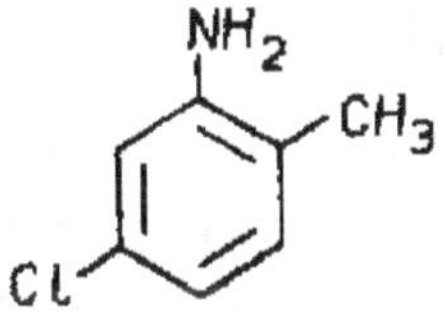
5	37125	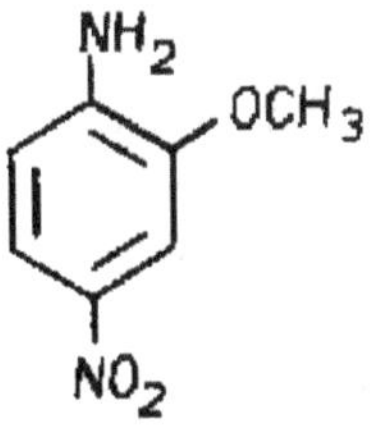
41	37165	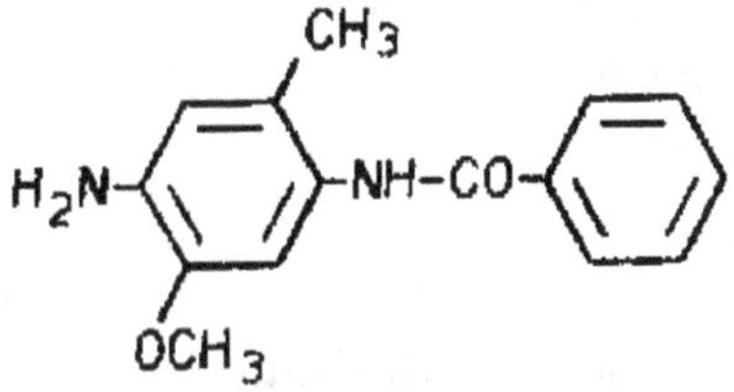
35	37255	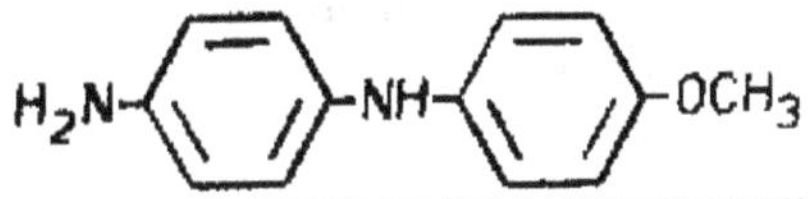

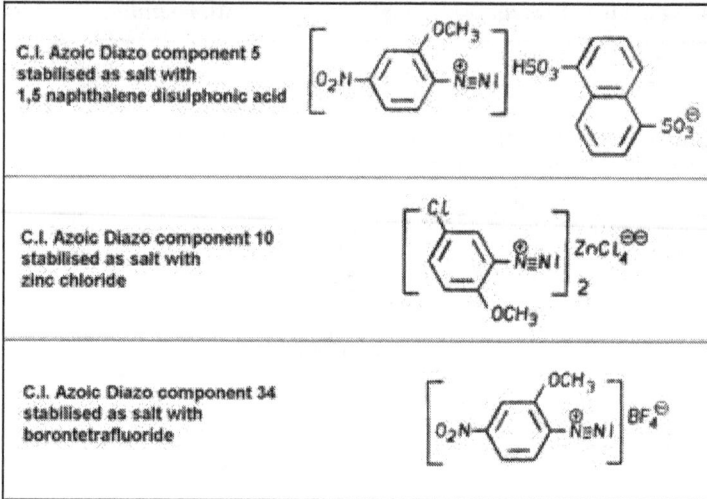

Figure 6.7: Typical Fast Colour Salts.

Naphthol Dyes (Azoic Dyes Developed on the Fibre)

Azoic dyes, also known as naphthol dyes, are used for cellulosic fibres (particularly cotton), but may also be applied to viscose, cellulose acetate, linen and sometimes polyester. Azoic dyes have excellent wet fastness properties as well as good light, chlorine and alkali fastness, while rubbing fastness is poor.

Chemical Characteristics and General Application Conditions

From a chemical point of view naphthol dyes are very similar to azo dyes, the main difference being the absence of sulphonic solubilising groups. They are made up of two chemically reactive compounds that are applied to the fabric in a two-stage process. The insoluble dye is synthesized directly in the fibre as the result of the coupling reaction between a diazotized base (developing agent) and a coupling component. The coupling components are usually derivatives of the anilides of the 2-hydroxy-3-naphthoic acid (also called naphthol AS). These naphthols are available in powder form or in liquid form (in this case the solution also contains caustic soda, the naphthol concentration ranges between 30 per cent and 60 per cent).

Developing agents can be derivatives of aniline, toluidine, ortho and meta-anisidine, diphenyl amine. They are available as:

☆ Free bases (fast colour bases).

☆ Liquid bases (these formulations are aqueous dispersions of the aromatic amines, they are safer and simpler to apply than solid bases).

☆ Fast colour salts (these are already diazotized diazonium compounds that are marketed in stabilized forms and do not need to be diazotized before use in dyeing.

Application of Azoic Colourants Involves a Number of Steps

☆ Preparation of the naphtholate solution: naphthol is converted to the naphtholates form to be able to couple with the diazonium salt.

☆ Application of the naphtholate to the fibre.

☆ Preparation of the diazotized base: in order to make the coupling reaction possible, the base must first be diazotized in the cold, using sodium nitrite and hydrochloric acid (this step can be avoided when using fast colour salts).

☆ Formation of the azoic dye into the fibre.

Environmental Issues

☆ **Aromatic amines:** Developing agents are all diazotisable amines or diamines or substituted anilines, toluidines, anisidines, azobenzenes or diphenylamines. Some of these amines and in particular, p-nitroaniline, chloroaniline and ß-naphtilamine are on the 1980 US EPA priority list as harmful pollutants and their use is forbidden.

☆ **Unfixed colourant:** Degree of fixation in continuous dyeing processes ranges between 76 and 89 per cent and between 80 and 91 per cent in printing processes

Reactive Dyes

Reactive dyes are mainly used for dyeing cellulose fibres such as cotton and viscose, but they are also increasingly gaining importance for wool and polyamide. They provide high wet fastness (better than the less expensive direct dyes), but their use is not always viable because of the difficulty in obtaining level dyeing. Chlorine fastness is slightly poorer than that of vat dyes, as is light fastness under severe conditions. The range of available reactive dyes is wide and enables a large number of dyeing techniques to be used.

Chemical Characteristics

Reactive dyes are unique in that they contain specific chemical groups capable of forming covalent links with the textile substrate. The energy required to break this bond is similar to that required to degrade the substrate itself, thus accounting for the high wet fastness of these dyes. The structure of Reactive Black 5, one of the most important reactive dyestuffs in terms of volumes consumed, is illustrated in Figure 6.8.

The reactive groups of the colourants react with the amino groups of the fibre in the case of protein and polyamide fibres, and with the hydroxyl groups in the case of cellulose. In both cases, depending on the anchor system, two reaction mechanisms are possible: a nucleophilic substitution mechanism or a nucleophilic addition mechanism. An important issue to consider when dealing with reactive dyes is the fact that two competing reactions are always involved in the colouring process:

1. **Alcoholysis:** dye + fibre ⟶ dye fixed on the fibre

$$NaO_3SO - CH_2 - CH_2 - SO_2 \text{—} \bigcirc \text{—} N{=}N \quad OH \quad NH_2 \quad N{=}N \text{—} \bigcirc \text{—} SO_2 - CH_2 - CH_2 - OSO_3Na$$

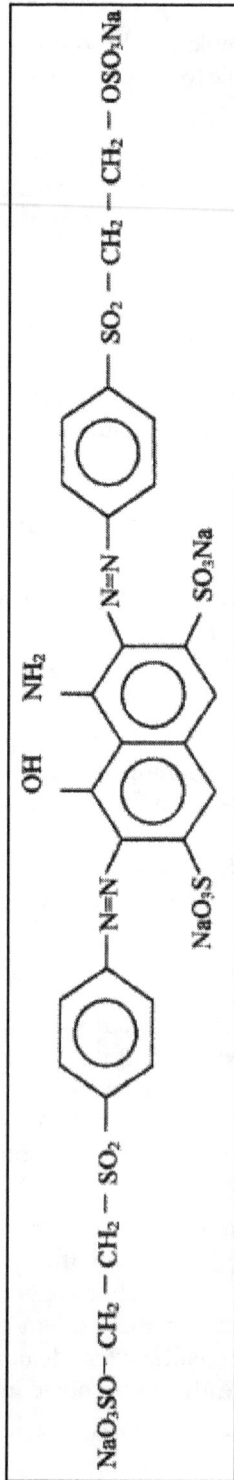

Figure 6.8: Chemical Structure of Reactive Black 5.

2. **Hydrolysis:** dye + water $\longrightarrow$ Hydrolyzed dye washed away after dyeing (undesired reaction)

This fact has important consequences, especially in the case of cellulose fibres. In fact, the alkaline conditions in which reactive dyes react with cellulose fibres which increase the rate of the hydrolysis reaction. The characteristics of the resulting hydrolyzed dye are such that the dye is no longer a reactive substance and it is therefore discharged in the effluent. Dyeing cellulose fibres with reactive dyes may imply the use of the following chemicals and auxiliaries:

☆ Alkali (sodium carbonate, bicarbonate and caustic soda)

☆ Salt (mainly sodium chloride and sulphate)

☆ Urea may be added to the padding liquor in continuous processes in the one-bath method

☆ Sodium silicate may be added in the cold pad-batch method

Reactive dyes are applied to wool or polyamide fibres under different conditions. In the case of wool and polyamide fibres, reactivity of the amino groups is considerably higher than that of hydroxyl groups in cellulose. Levelling properties are often achieved with the use of speciality amphoteric leveling agents. Reactive dyes are generally applied at pH values of between 4.5 and 7, depending on depth of shade, in the presence of ammonium sulphate and the specialized leveling agents mentioned above. In cellulose printing, moderately reactive dyes are generally employed (mainly mono chloro triazine systems). Highly reactive sulphoethyl sulphones are also sometimes used. Printing with reactive dyes requires the use of:

☆ Thickening agents (mainly polyacrylates in combination with alginates)

☆ Urea

☆ Alkali (*e.g.* sodium carbonate and bicarbonate)

☆ Oxidising agents (mainly benzene sulphonic acid derivatives): they are used to prevent reduction of more sensitive dyes during steaming.

Environmental Issues

Poor dye fixation has been a long-standing problem with reactive dyes in particular in batch dyeing of cellulose fibres, where a significant amount of salt is normally added to improve dye exhaustion (and therefore also dye fixation). On the other hand, shade reproducibility and level dyeing was the major obstacle in production using the most efficient dyes (high exhaustion and fixation rate). Research and development has been faced with a number of objectives, all of which have been or are in the process of being successfully achieved.

☆ Increasing the robustness of individual dyes and dye combinations (trichromatic systems)

☆ Enhancing reproducibility of trichromatic combinations used in most commonly applied dyeing processes

☆ Reducing salt consumption and/or unused dye in the effluent

☆ Improving fastness properties (*e.g.* light fastness, fastness to repeated laundering).

With the use of sophisticated molecular engineering techniques it has been possible to design reactive dyes (*e.g.* bi-functional dyes and low-salt reactive dyes) with considerably higher performances than traditional reactive dyes.

☆ **Bio-eliminability:** Because both unfixed reactive dye and its hydrolyzed form are readily soluble they are difficult to eliminate in biological waste water treatment plants.

☆ **Organic halogens:** Many reactive dyes contain organic halogens. However, a distinction has to be made between halogens bonded to the chromophore and halogens bonded to the anchor group.

☆ **Heavy metals:** Heavy metals can be present both as impurities from the production process (limits have been set by ETAD) and as an integral part of the chromophore. The latter concerns phthalocyanine dyes, which are still widely used especially for blue and turquoise shades (substitutes have not yet been found).

☆ **Unfixed colourant:** Fixation rate can be poor. Efforts have been made to increase the level of fixation. Some reactive dyes can reach >95 per cent of fixation even for Cellulosic fibres.

Sulphur Dyes

Sulphur dyes are mainly used for cotton and viscose substrates. They may also be used for dyeing blends of cellulose and synthetic fibres, including polyamides and polyesters. They are occasionally used for dyeing silk. Apart from black shades, sulphur dyes play almost no part in textile printing. Bleach and wash fastness properties are very good, while light fastness varies from moderate to good. Although they encompass a broad shade range, sulphur dyes are mostly used for dark shades because lighter shades have poor resistance to light and laundering. Sulphur dyes tend to be dull compared with other dye classes.

Chemical Characteristics and General Application Conditions

Sulphur dyes are made up of high molecular weight compounds, obtained by reaction of sulphur or sulphides with amines and phenols. Many colourant exist that contain sulphur in their molecule, but only dyestuffs which become soluble in water after reaction with sodium sulphide under alkaline conditions can be called sulphur dyes. The exact chemical structure is not always known because these are mixtures of molecules of a high level of complexity. Amino derivatives, nitro benzenes, nitro and amino biphenyls, substituted phenols, substituted naphthalene, condensed aromatic compounds, indophenols, azines, oxazine, thiazol, azine and thiazine rings can be part of these compounds. Sulphur dyes contain sulphur both as an integral part of the chromophore and in polysulphide side chains. As has already been mentioned, sulphur dyes are insoluble in water, but after reduction under alkaline conditions they are converted into the leuco form, which is water-soluble and has high affinity for the fibre. After absorption into the fibre they are oxidized and converted to the original insoluble state. Sulphur dyes are available in various modifications, which are classified under the following names:

☆ **Sulphur dyes:** Available as amorphous powders or dispersible pigments. Amorphous powders are insoluble or partially soluble in water and are brought into solution by boiling with sodium sulphide and water. Dispersible pigments can be used in this form for pad dyeing in presence of a dispersing agent. They can contain a certain amount of reducing agent already in the formulation and in this case are called "partly reduced pigments".

☆ **Leuco-sulphur dyes (ready-for-use dyes):** Available in liquid form and already contain the reducing agent required for dyeing. Therefore they must simply be diluted with water before application. Low-sulphide types are also available on the market.

☆ **Water-soluble sulphur dyes:** Available in the form of Bunte salts (Col-S-SO_3Na) obtained by treating the dye in its insoluble form (Col-S-S-Col) with sodium hydro-sulphite. They can be dissolved in hot water, but they do not have affinity for the fibre. The addition of alkali and reducing agent makes them substantive for the fibre.

Sodium sulphide and sodium hydrogen sulphide are generally employed as reducing agents to bring into solution the dye (unless ready-for-use sulphur dyes are applied). Binary systems made of glucose and sodium dithionite (hydro-sulphite) or thio-urea dioxides are also used as alternative reducing agents. In all processes the dye is finally fixed on the substrate by oxidation. Now-a-days, hydrogen peroxide or halogen-containing compounds such as bromate, iodate and chlorite are the most commonly used oxidizing agents. Apart from the above-mentioned reducing and oxidizing agents, additional chemicals and auxiliaries required when dyeing with sulphur dyes are:

☆ Alkali (mainly caustic soda)

☆ Salt (sodium chloride and sulphate)

☆ **Dispersing agents:** Usually they are naphthalene sulphonic acid-formaldehyde condensates, lignin sulphonates and sulphonated oils

☆ **Complexing agents:** EDTA and polyphosphates are used in some cases to prevent negative effects due to the presence of alkaline-earth ions.

Environmental Issues

☆ **Bio-eliminability:** Most Sulphur dyes are water-insoluble after oxidation and therefore they can largely be eliminated by adsorption on the activated sludge in the waste water treatment plant.

☆ **Unfixed colourant:** Degree of fixation ranges between 60 and 90 per cent in continuous dyeing and 65 - 95 per cent in printing.

☆ **Effluent contamination:** By additives in the dye formulation, poorly biodegradable dispersants are present. New formaldehyde condensation products with higher elimination (>70 per cent) are already available.

Vat Dyes

Vat dyes are used most often in dyeing and printing of cotton and cellulose fibres. They can also be applied for dyeing polyamide and polyester blends with cellulose fibres. Vat dyes have excellent fastness properties when properly selected and are often used for fabrics that will be subjected to severe washing and bleaching conditions (toweling, industrial and military uniforms, etc.). The range of colours is wide, but shades are generally dull.

Chemical Characteristics and General Application Conditions

From a chemical point of view, vat dyes can be distinguished into two groups: indigoid vat dyes and anthraquinoid dyes. Indigo dyes are almost exclusively used for dyeing warp yarn in the production of blue denim. Like sulphur dyes, vat dyes are normally insoluble in water, but they become water-soluble and substantive for the fibre after reduction in alkaline conditions (vatting). They are then converted again to the original insoluble form by oxidation and in this way they remain fixed into the fibre. Vat dyes are preparations that basically consist of a vattable coloured pigment and a dispersing agent (mainly formaldehyde condensation products and lignin sulphonates). They are generally supplied in powder, granules and paste form.

A wide range of different techniques are used in colouring processes with vat dyes. Nevertheless, all processes involve three steps:

- ☆ Vatting
- ☆ Oxidation
- ☆ After treatment.

The step in which the reduction of the dyestuff into its leuco-form takes place is called vatting. Vat dyes are generally more difficult to reduce than sulphur dyes. Various reducing agents are used. Sodium dithionite (hydro-sulphite) is still the most widely employed although it has some limits. Sodium dithionite is consumed by reduction of the dye and also by reaction with atmospheric oxygen, therefore an excess of reducing agent has to be used and various techniques have been proposed to reduce these losses. The typical examples of vat dyes are shown in Figure 6.9.

In addition sodium dithionite cannot be used for high temperature or pad-steam dyeing processes because over-reduction can occur with sensitive dyes. In these application conditions and also for printing, sulphoxylic acid derivatives are normally preferred. Thio urea dioxide is also sometimes used as a reducing agent, but a risk of over-reduction exists as its reduction potential is much higher than that of hydro sulphite. Furthermore the oxidation products of thio-urea dioxide contribute to nitrogen and sulphur contamination of waste water.

Following increasing environmental pressures, biodegradable sulphur-free organic reducing agents such as hydro xyacetone are now available. Their reducing effect, however, is weaker than that of hydro sulphite, so they cannot replace it in all applications. Nevertheless hydroxy acetone can be used in combination with hydro sulphite, thus reducing to a certain extent the sulphite load in the effluent.

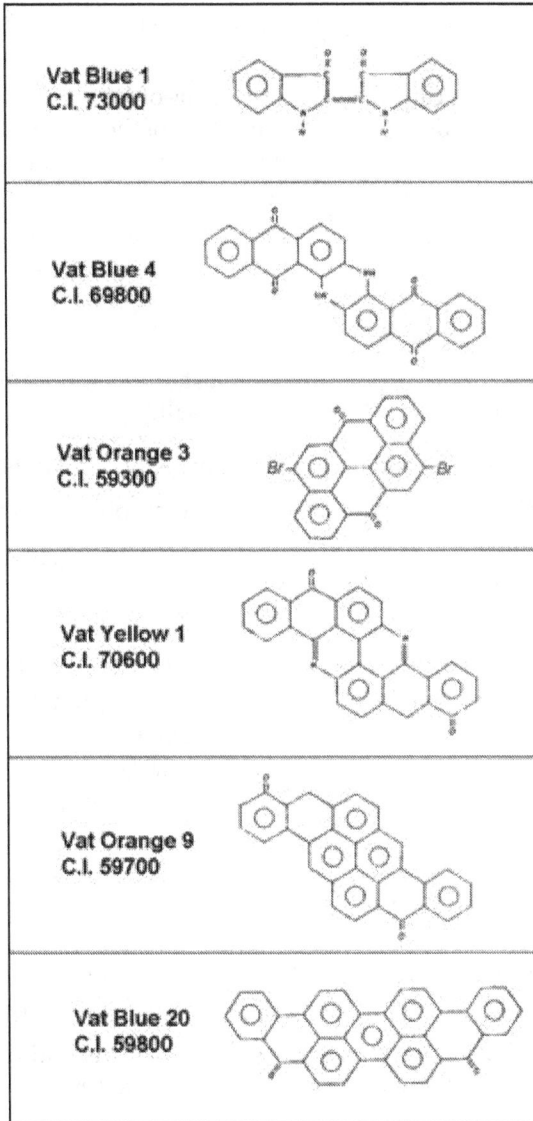

Figure 6.9: Typical Vat Dyes.

After absorption by the fibre, the dye in its soluble leuco form is converted to the original pigment by **oxidation**. This process is carried out in the course of wet treatment (washing) by addition of oxidants such as hydrogen peroxide, perborate or 3-nitrobenzenesulphonic acid to the liquor.

The final step consists in **after-treating** the material in weakly alkaline liquor with a detergent at boiling temperature. This soap treatment is not only aimed at removing pigment particles, but also allows the crystallization of amorphous dye particles, which gives the material the final shade and the fastness properties typical of vat dyes.

Vat dyeing conditions can vary widely in terms of temperature and the amount of salt and alkali required, depending on the nature of the dye applied. Vat dyes are therefore divided into the following groups, according to their affinity for the fibre and the amount of alkali required for dyeing:

- ☆ IK dyes (I = Indanthren, K = cold) have low affinity, they are dyed at 20 - 30°C and require little alkali and salt to increase dye absorption.
- ☆ IW dyes (W = warm) have higher affinity; they are dyed at 40 - 45°C with more alkali and little or no salt.
- ☆ IN dyes (N = normal) are highly substantive and applied at 60°C and require much alkali, but no addition of salt.

The following chemicals and auxiliaries may be found in dyeing processes:

- ☆ Sodium dithionite, thiourea dioxide and sulphoxilic acid derivatives as reducing agents
- ☆ Caustic soda
- ☆ Sodium sulphate
- ☆ Polyacrylates and alginates as anti-migration agents in padding processes
- ☆ Formaldehyde condensation products with naphthalene sulphonic acid and lignin sulphonates as dispersing agents
- ☆ Surfactants (including ethoxylated fatty amines) and other components such as betaines, polyalkylen amines, polyvinyl pyrolidine as levelling agents
- ☆ Hydrogen peroxide, perborate, 3-nitrobenzenesulphonic acid as oxidants
- ☆ Soap.

The following chemicals and auxiliaries may be found in printing processes:

- ☆ Thickening agents (starch esters with seed flour derivatives)
- ☆ **Reducing agents:** Various chemicals are used depending on the printing method (all-in or two-phase process), dye selected and steaming conditions. Sulphoxylic acid derivatives are the most common, but hydrosulphite can also be used (in the two-phase process when very short steaming time is required)
- ☆ **Alkali:** Potassium carbonate, sodium carbonate, sodium hydroxide
- ☆ Oxidising agents (the same used for dyeing)
- ☆ Soap.

Environmental Issues

- ☆ **Bio-eliminability:** Vat dyes can be regarded as highly eliminable due to the fact that they are water-insoluble and therefore largely adsorbed on the activated sludge in the waste water treatment plant.

☆ **Eco-toxicity:** Since they are sparingly soluble they are not bio-available.

☆ **Heavy metals:** Vat dyes contain heavy metal impurities (Cu, Fe, Mn, Ba and Pb) due to their production process (in some cases it is still difficult to keep these limits below the ETAD standards).

☆ **Unfixed colourant:** Vat dyes show high exhaustion levels (70 - 95 per cent in continuous dyeing processes and 70 - 80 per cent in printing).

☆ **Effluent contamination:** By additives in the dye formulation, Dispersants are present in the dye formulation. As they are water-soluble and poorly degradable, they are found in the waste water. New formaldehyde condensation products with higher elimination (>70 per cent) are already available and more readily eliminable substitutes are being developed.

7

Dyeing: Machinery and Techniques

Loose Fibre - Autoclave

Various types of machines are used for processing fibres in loose form. These include conical pan machines, pear-shaped machines and radial flow machines. They are used for all wet operations, that is, pretreatment, dyeing, application of finishing agents and washing. The typical fibre dyeing autoclave machine is shown in Figure 7.1.

In conical pan machines the fibre is packed into a removable fibre carrier, which is located onto a central spigot in the base of the vessel. Liquor circulation is provided, via this connection, by an external pump. Associated pipe work allows liquor to be circulated either from the base of the pack or from the top. Pear-shapes machines have a removable perforated base plate through which liquor is circulated via an impeller, returning to the dyeing vessel via a weir. Fibre is loaded directly into these machines and a further perforated plate is positioned on top. Liquor circulation packs the fibre into the base of the machine between the two plates. To unload the machine both plates are removed by crane and the fibre is manually removed.

Radial flow machines are characterized by a fibre carrier, equipped with a central perforated column from which liquor flows across the pack to the perforated walls of the carrier. Loose fibre is typically packed into these machines manually. Capacity varies between 200 - 300 kg, with a working volume equivalent to between 7 and 10 liters per kg fibre. The low packing density in these machines allows liquor to circulate freely through the fibre pack at modest pressures, thus minimizing mechanical damage to the fibre while ensuring level dyeing. The bath is heated by closed steam coils in the base of the machine. In many cases the level of automation on these machines is

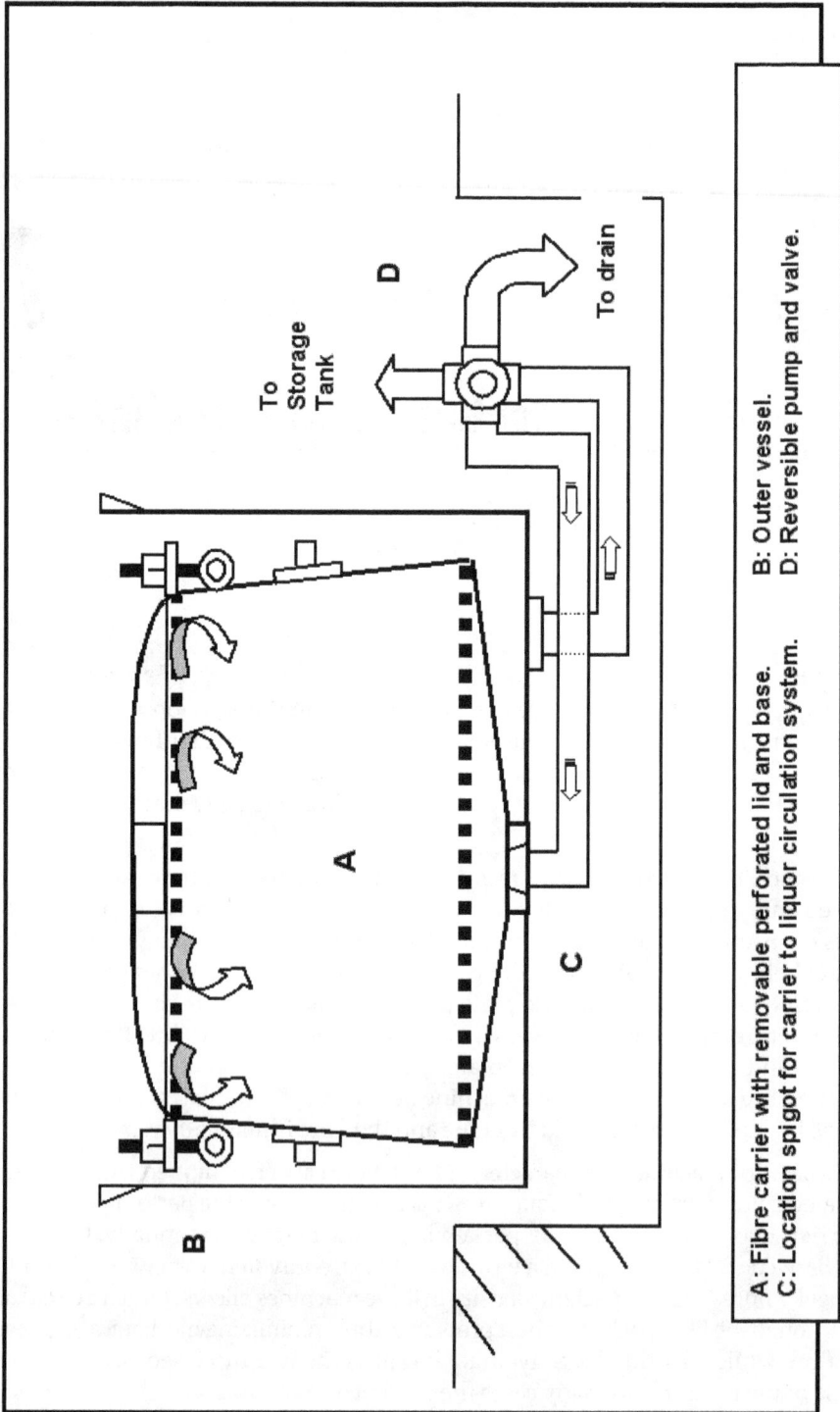

Figure 7.1: Fibre Dyeing Autoclave Machine.

A: Fibre carrier with removable perforated lid and base.   B: Outer vessel.
C: Location spigot for carrier to liquor circulation system.   D: Reversible pump and valve.

low and temperature may be controlled manually with a simple steam valve. In other cases electro/pneumatic programmers or logic controllers may be installed to regulate time/temperature and to control the direction of liquor circulation.

Autoclaves can be equipped for operation at higher pressure (this is not the case when they are used for dyeing wool fibres). Autoclaves of all designs may be fitted with an external holding tank, capable of accommodating at least the volume of the dyeing vessel. Such tanks are used to facilitate re-use of liquors in more than one dyeing. Occasionally more than one dyeing vessel may be connected to a common tank, allowing liquor to be shared between vessels. The liquor ratio for loose fibre can vary between 1:4 to 1:12, depending on the type of machine, level of loading, type of fibre, etc.

Yarn

Yarn can be processed either in hank form or in package. Different machines are used depending on the method chosen. They are used for all wet operations, that is, pretreatment, dyeing, application of finishing agents and washing.

Hank Dyeing Machines

Hank dyeing machines are mostly of the single stick design, in which hanks are hung from the underside of the dyeing vessel lid on removable sticks. The construction of hank dyeing machine is shown in Figure 7.2. The lid is lowered vertically onto the dyeing vessel, which consists of a simple box with a perforated false bottom. Liquor is circulated by a reversible impeller, located vertically in a weir chamber at one end of the machine. Heating is typically by closed steam coils beneath the false bottom and on smaller machines by live steam injection. Temperature control is provided by electro-mechanical or programmable logic controllers. These devices may also control/ time the timing of chemical and dye additions and any required cooling cycles. Machine capacities vary from 10 kg sample machines to 1000 kg machines. These larger machines may be coupled together in pairs with interconnecting pipe work in such a way that yarn loads of up to 4000 kg can be dyed while still retaining the flexibility to dye individual 1000 kg lots. Variations of this design may utilize a horizontal circulation impeller passing through a sealing gland at the base of the weir chamber. Such machines invariably have a concave bottom, which is said to improve circulation and reduce fibre to liquor ratio by a small margin. Liquor ratios from 1:15 to 1:25 are typical for these machines.

Package Dyeing Machines

Three basic types of machine may be used for package dyeing wool yarns: horizontal or vertical spindle machines or tube type machines.

☆ **Horizontal spindle machines** may be rectangular in design, similar to hank dyeing machines, but modified to take frames, onto which yarn packages are inserted horizontally, or alternatively may be a horizontal autoclave into which is wheeled the carrier containing the yarn packages. Both types operate with high flow rate pumps, which are necessary to give good circulation of the dye liquor. These machines are usually used for bulky

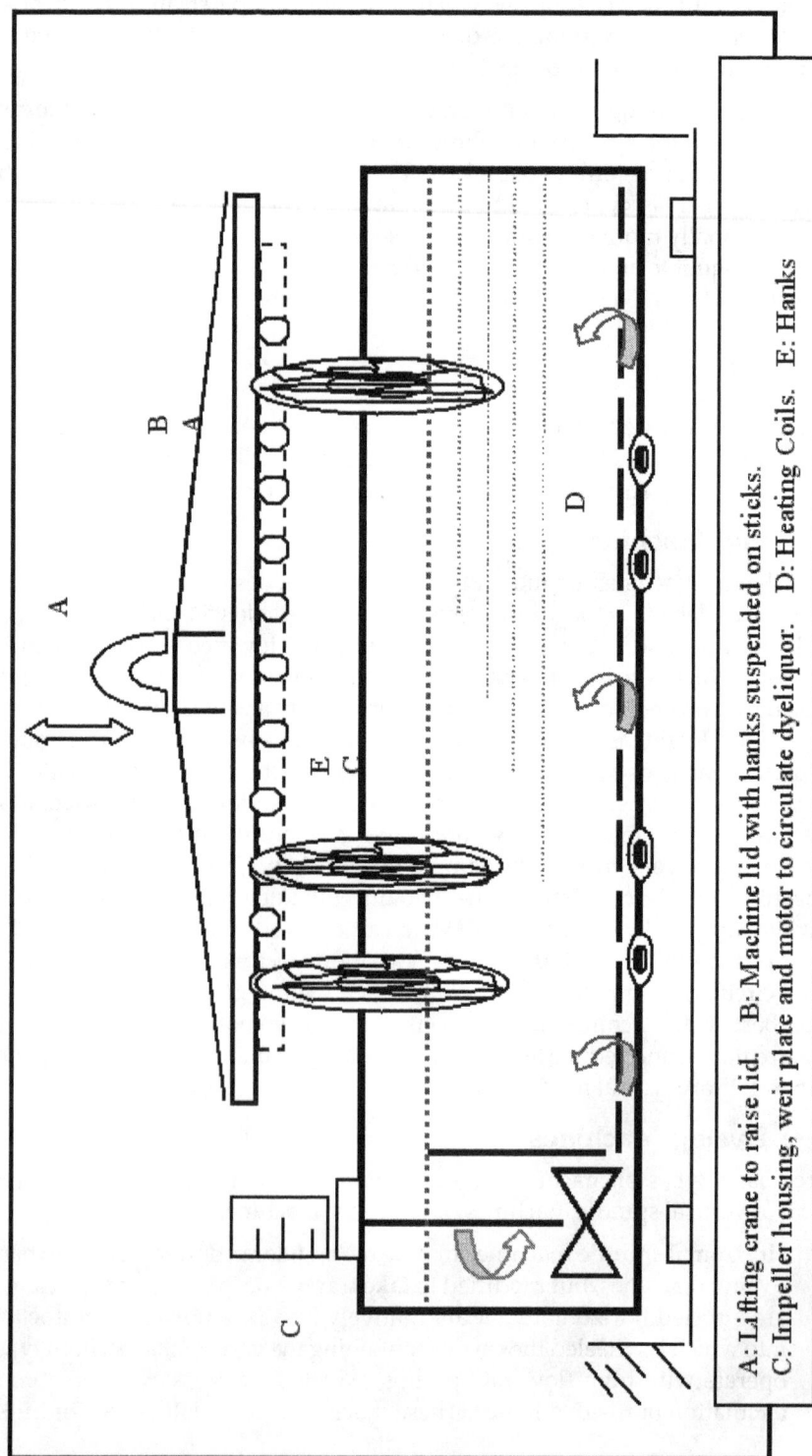

A: Lifting crane to raise lid.   B: Machine lid with hanks suspended on sticks.
C: Impeller housing, weir plate and motor to circulate dyeliquor.   D: Heating Coils.   E: Hanks

Figure 7.2 Hank Dyeing machine

yarns, which are wound onto soft packages, again to increase dye liquor penetration.

☆ **Vertical spindle machines** are the most commonly used. The packages may be press packed onto vertical carrier spindles to increase payload, assist in dye liquor circulation and minimize liquor to fibre ratio.

☆ **Tube type machines** shown in Figure 7.3 consist of a number of vertical or horizontal tubes into which package carriers are inserted, the tubes forming individual dyeing vessels linked by common pipe work and circulation pumps. These machines are more flexible than the above types because individual tubes can be blanked off to vary the overall load capacity of the machine.

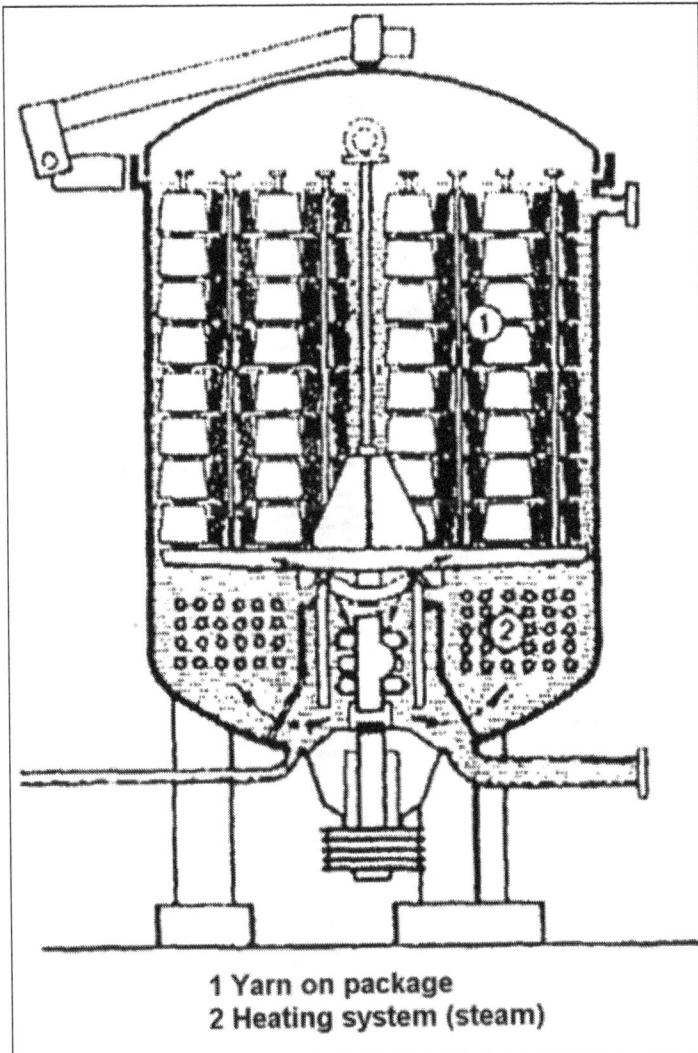

1 Yarn on package
2 Heating system (steam)

Figure 7.3: Tube Type Package Dyeing Machine.

☆ **Liquor ratios** employed in package dyeing are close to 1:12 (typically from 1:8 to 1:15). Machines with capacities of up to 500 kg are used in dyeing carpet yarns, with the facility to link two or more machine together when dyeing larger single batches.

Fabric in Rope Form

Wet treatments on fabrics in rope form can be carried out both in batch and in continuous processes.

Batch Processes

Winch Beck

The common element in all winch beck machines is the winch mechanism which is used to move the fabric. The winch dyeing machine is shown in Figure 7.4. The winch draws the fabric via a guide roller out of the bath and returns it in folds into the bath. In the conventional winch beck, the bath stands still, while the fabric is kept in circulation by a reel positioned in the upper part of the machine. In modern winches both the bath and the fabric are kept in circulation, which improves homogenization

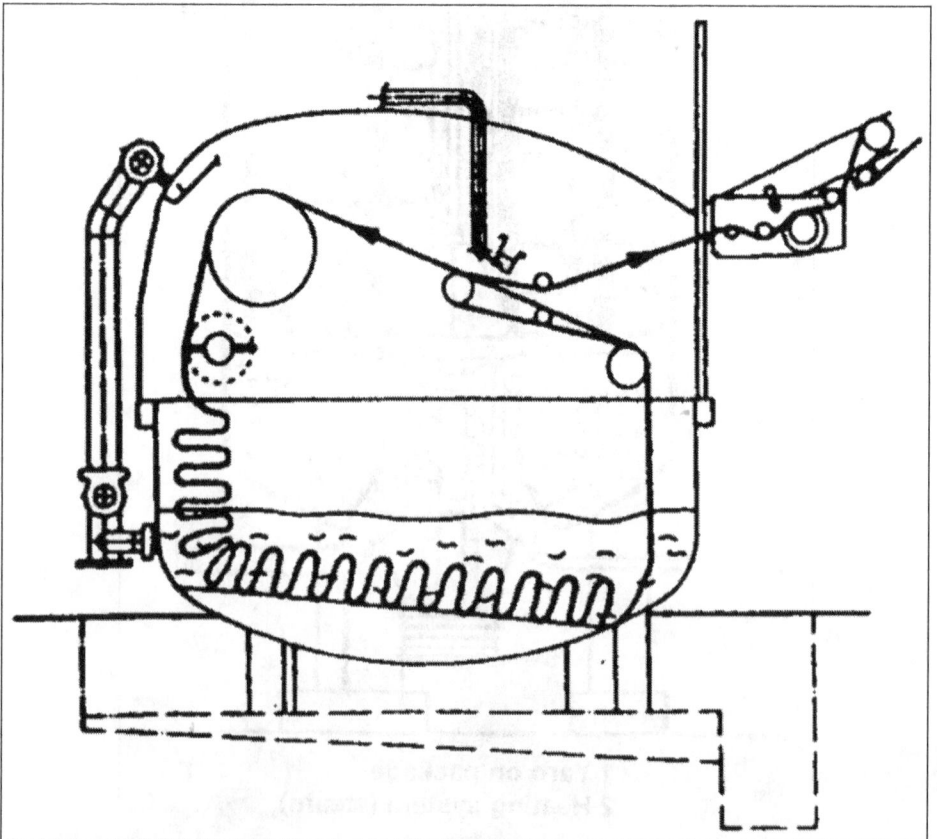

Figure 7.4: Winch Dyeing Machine.

and exchange of the liquor with the fabric. Goods are loaded into the winch either in rope form or in open width, which means that the winches must be 5 - 6 metres in width. The ends of the fabric piece to be dyed are sewn together to form endless loops over the rotating boom (winch). Winch becks are primarily machines for dyeing, but for practical reasons both preparation and dyeing are normally carried out in the same machine.

These machines are essentially operated at atmospheric pressure although the development of synthetic fibres has led to the production of pressurized machines (HT machines may reach 130 - 140°C). Winch beck is a very versatile machine and it can be used for all types of fabric. It is a very common technique for dyeing carpets (they are usually dyed in full width). Typical bath ratios vary from 1:15 to 1:40 (typically 1:30 in the carpet sector)], which makes this technique fairly expensive due to high water and energy consumption. However, recent technological developments have been made to improve its environmental performance.

Jet Dyeing Machine

The construction of jet dyeing machine is shown in Figure 7.5. Jet machines have been designed with the aim of eliminating some of the problems associated with the use of winch machines. The reel is eliminated and the fabric is placed in a closed tubular system. A jet of dye liquor is supplied through a venture to transport the fabric through the tube. Turbulence created by the jet aids in dye penetration and

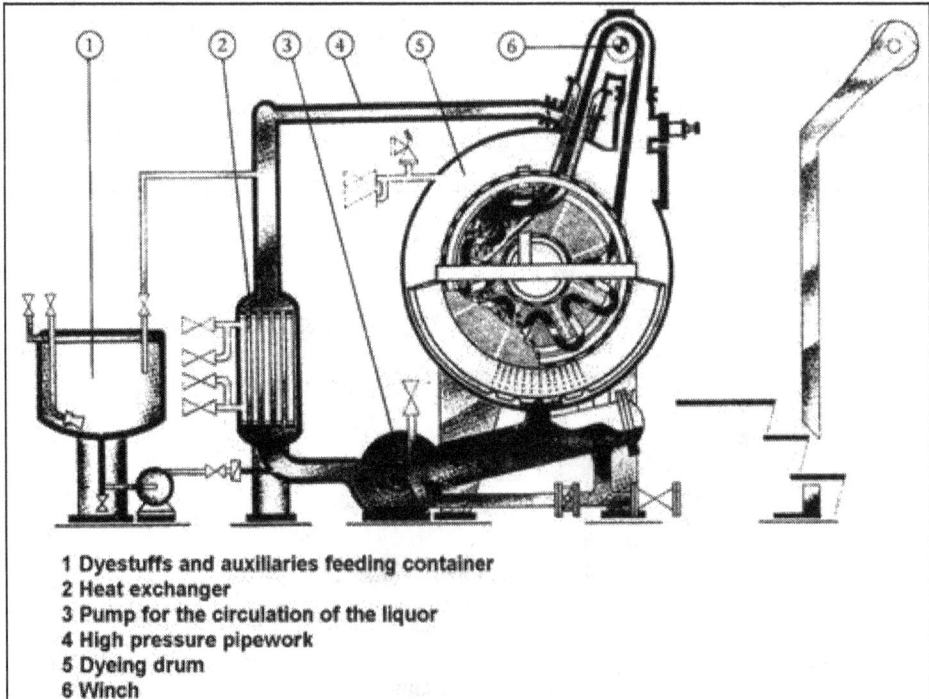

1 Dyestuffs and auxiliaries feeding container
2 Heat exchanger
3 Pump for the circulation of the liquor
4 High pressure pipework
5 Dyeing drum
6 Winch

Figure 7.5: Jet Dyeing Machine.

prevents the fabric from touching the walls of the tube. Since the fabric is frequently exposed to high liquor concentrations within the transport tube, relatively little dye bath is needed in the bottom of the vessel: just enough to ensure smooth movement from rear to front.

Advantages of this machine are therefore low consumption of water and short treatment time (*e.g.* short dyeing time). Typical liquor ratios vary between 1:4 and 1:20, ranging from 1:4 to 1:10 for fabric and from 1:6 to 1:20 for carpet (lower values apply to synthetic fibres while higher values are typical for cotton). Jets can usually be operated at high temperatures, which make them very suitable for dyeing polyester fibres. A disadvantage, however, is the high mechanical stress on the textile, caused by the speed difference between the bath and the fabric. For this reason jets are not suitable for some delicate fabrics. Depending on the shape of the fabric storage area (long shape machine or J-box compact machine), the type of nozzle and its position (above or below the level of the bath) various types of jets exist. Overflow, soft-flow and airflow dyeing machines can be regarded as developments of the conventional jet. The main features of these machines are reported in the following sections.

Overflow

The material passage in overflow dyeing machines is shown in Figure 7.6. Overflows have been designed for delicate knitted and woven fabrics made of natural and synthetic fibres. They are also found in the carpet sector. The main difference between jet and overflows machines remains in the fact that in jet machines the fabric is transported by the bath flowing at high speed through the nozzle, while with overflows the fabric is transported by the gravitational force of the liquor overflow.

A winch (usually not motor driven) is located in the upper part of the machine and the fabric hangs over it. A longer length of textile hangs from the exit side of the winch than from the inlet side. Gravitational forces pull the longer length of textile

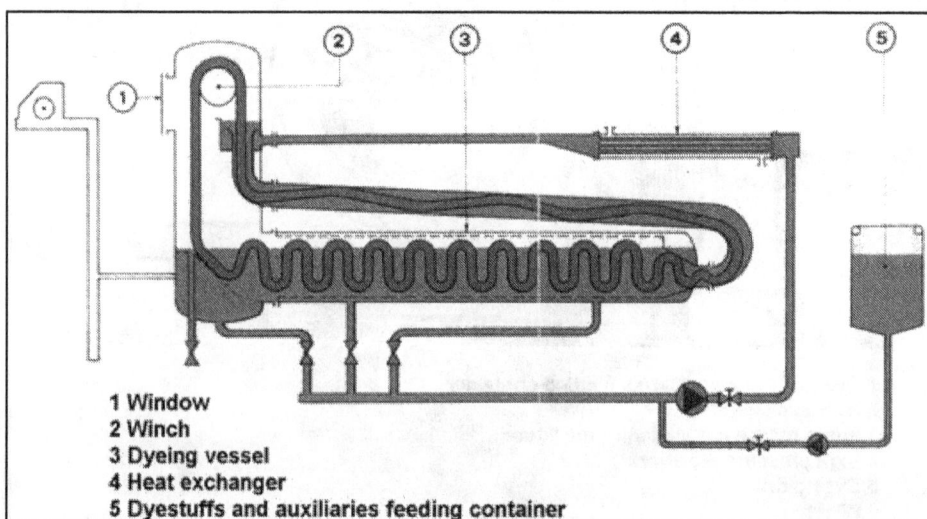

1 Window
2 Winch
3 Dyeing vessel
4 Heat exchanger
5 Dyestuffs and auxiliaries feeding container

Figure 7.6: Overflow Dyeing Machine.

downward more strongly than the shorter. The fabric is therefore soaked in the bath without any tension (transportation is very gentle). Different designs are available on the market and some of them can operate under pressure and consequently at higher temperatures. Typical liquor ratios for overflows range between 1:12 and 1:20.

Soft-flow

The so-called "soft-flow" machines use the same transport tube principle as overflow machines where the fabric is transported in a stream of dye liquor. However, while in overflow machines the reel is not motor driven, in soft-flow equipment the reel and the jet work in constant harmony to remove the fabric from the front of the storage area, expose it briefly to a high concentration of liquor within the transport tube, then return it to the rear of the vessel. The soft flow machines are gentler on the fabric than conventional jet overflow machines.

Continuous Processes

Machines for treatment in continuous processes of fabrics in rope form are essentially composed of the following parts:

☆ A padding device for impregnating the fabric in rope form

☆ A storage area for the fixation of the chemicals applied

☆ A washing machine for fabric in rope form.

The padding device is composed of a long basin equipped with two or three rotating rollers at the inlet and another two at the outlet. The basin contains a concentrated solution of the chemicals and auxiliaries that have to be applied (desizing agents, bleaching agents, etc.). The fabric is pressed by the rotating rollers at the inlet in order to obtain a homogeneous absorption of the chemicals and the elimination of air. The other two rollers only squeeze the fabric. After squeezing, the fabric retains only a relatively low amount of bath. As a result high concentrations of the chemicals are needed; moreover the solutions must be adequately stabilized to avoid unwanted oxidation reactions, etc. The storage area (also called reaction chamber) can have different shapes: one typical model is the J-Box. The J-Box is filled to 1/3 of its capacity with the treatment bath. The main advantage of this technique is the high production capacity. On the other hand there is the risk of longitudinal creases, which can negatively affect the dyeing process. As a result this technique is mainly applied for white end-products for pretreatment operations (*e.g.* bleaching).

Airflow

The difference between air jet and jet machines is that in the former an air jet instead of a water jet keeps the fabric in circulation. The fabric passes into the storage area which contains a very small amount of free liquor. As a result, a reduction in water, energy and chemicals consumption can be achieved. Because of the short liquor ratios achievable (from 1:2 to 1:5) the dye must be highly water-soluble.

8

Printing

Printing, like dyeing, is a process for applying colour to a substrate. However, instead of colouring the whole substrate (cloth, carpet or yarn) as in dyeing, print colour is applied only to defined areas to obtain the desired pattern. This involves different techniques and different machinery with respect to dyeing, but the physical and chemical processes that take place between the dye and the fibre are analogous to dyeing.

Printing Process Steps

A typical printing process involves the following steps:

- ☆ **Colour paste preparation:** When printing textiles, the dye or pigment is not in aqueous liquor, instead, it is usually finely dispersed in a printing paste, in high concentration.

- ☆ **Printing:** The dye or pigment paste is applied to the substrate using different techniques, which are discussed below.

- ☆ **Fixation:** Immediately after printing, the fabric is dried and then the prints are fixed mainly with steam or hot air (for pigments). Note that intermediate drying is not carried out when printing carpets (too much energy would be needed for removing the highly viscous liquor).

- ☆ **After-treatment:** This final operation consists in washing and drying the fabric (it is not necessary when printing with pigments or with other particular techniques such as transfer printing).

When describing the different printing techniques, a distinction should be made between printing with pigments, which have no affinity for the fibre, and printing with dyes (reactive, vat, disperse, etc.).

Printing with Pigments

Pigment printing has gained much importance today and for some fibres (*e.g.* cellulose fibres) is by far the most commonly applied technique. Pigments can be used on almost all types of textile substrates and, thanks to increased performance of modern auxiliaries; it is now possible to obtain high-quality printing using this technique. Pigment printing pastes contain a thickening agent, a binder and, if necessary, other auxiliaries such as fixing agents, plasticizers, defoamers, etc. White spirit-based emulsions, used in the past as thickening systems, are used only occasionally today (mainly half-emulsion thickeners). After applying the printing paste, the fabric is dried and then the pigment is normally fixed with hot air (depending on the type of binder in the formulation, fixation can also be achieved by storage at 20°C for a few days). The advantage of pigment printing is that the process can be done without subsequent washing (which, in turn, is needed for most of the other printing techniques).

Printing with Dyes

Printing Paste Preparation

The process traditionally starts with the preparation of the paste. Compared to pigment printing, the composition of the pastes is more complex and variable, being determined not by the dye used, but by the printing technique, the substrate, the application and the fixation methods applied.

Apart from the dye, printing pastes contain a thickening agent and various other auxiliaries, which can be classified according to their function as follows:

☆ Oxidising agents (*e.g.* *m*-nitrobenzene sulphonate, sodium chlorate, hydrogen peroxide)

☆ Reducing agents (*e.g.* sodium dithionite, formaldehyde sulphoxylates, thiourea dioxide, tin(II) chloride)

☆ Discharging agents for discharge printing (*e.g.* anthraquinone)

☆ Substances with a hydrotropic effect, like urea

☆ Dye solubilisers, which are polar organic solvents like glycerine, ethylen glycol, butyl glycol, thiodiglycol, etc.

☆ Resists for reactive resist printing (*e.g.* sulphonated alkanes)

☆ Defoamers, (*e.g.* silicon compounds, organic and inorganic esters, aliphatic esters, etc.).

All the necessary ingredients are metered (dosed) and mixed together in a mixing station. Since between 5 and 10 different printing pastes are usually necessary to print a single pattern (in some cases up to 20 different pastes are applied), in order to reduce losses, due to incorrect measurement, the preparation of the pastes is done in automatic stations. In modern plants, with the help of special devices, the exact amount of printing paste required is determined and prepared in continuous mode for each printing position, thus reducing leftovers at the end of the run. It is common practice in many printing houses to filter the printing pastes before application, using for example a filter cloth. This operation is especially important for thickeners to prevent free particles from blocking the openings of the screens.

Printing (Paste Application)

After preparation, the paste is applied to specific areas of the textile using one of the following techniques:

☆ Direct printing (which also includes digital and transfer printing)

☆ Discharge printing

☆ Resist printing.

In the case of direct printing the dye is applied to specific areas of a pretreated textile substrate, which can be white or pre-dyed (in light colours).

The fixation process in discharge printing is shown in Figure 8.1. It is possible to speak of discharge printing, if in the fixation process that follows the application of the printing paste there is local destruction of a dye applied previously. If the etched (discharge), previously dyed area becomes white, then the process is called white discharge. If, on the contrary, a coloured pattern has to be obtained in the etched area after the destruction of the previously applied dye, then the process is called coloured discharge. In this case the printing paste must contain a reduction-resistant dye along with the chemicals needed to destroy the previous one. As a result the pre-dyed background is destroyed according to a pattern and the dye, which is resistant to reduction, takes its place.

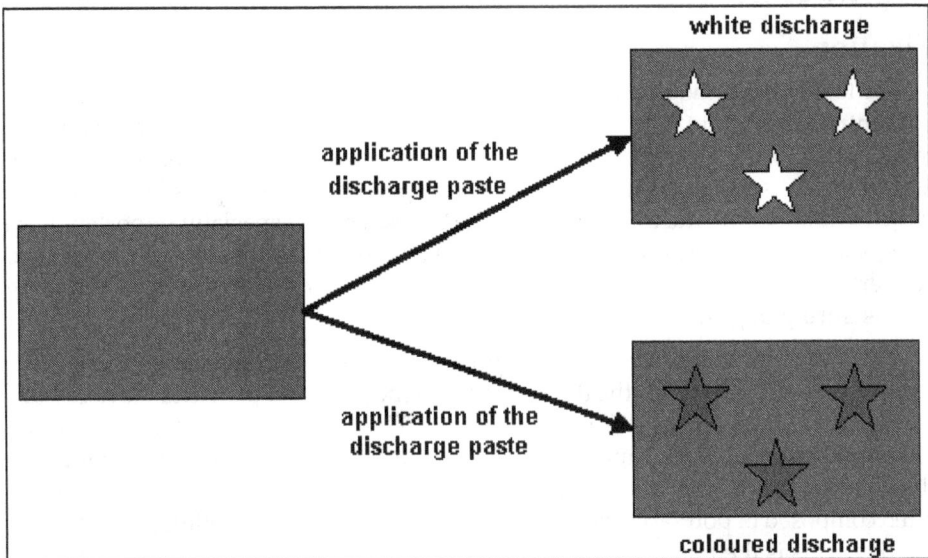

Figure 8.1: Schematic Representation of Discharge Printing.

In the case of resist printing, a special printing paste (called «resist») is printed onto certain areas of the fabric to prevent dye fixation. The process of resist printing is shown in Figure 8.2. In the case of physical resist the material is printed with a difficult-to-wet resin that inhibits the penetration of a dye applied in a second stage. On the other hand, with a chemical resist, dye fixation is prevented by a chemical reaction. Depending on the way the process is carried out, one can speak of pre-printing, intermediate or over-printing resists. One common procedure is the wet-on-wet process in which the resist paste is initially printed, then the material is overprinted with full cover screen and finally fixed and washed. Over-printing resists can be applied only if the dye, already present in the previously dyed and dried fabric, is still in its unfixed form, as in the case of developing dyes.

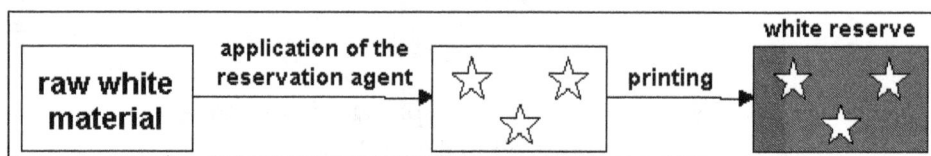

Figure 8.2: Schematic Representation of Resist Printing.

The difference between transfer printing and the techniques described earlier is that with this technique the surface of the fabric is not directly printed. Instead, the pattern is first created on an intermediate carrier (*e.g.* paper) using selected disperse dyes and then it is transferred from there to the fabric. The dye is usually fixed by placing the printed paper in contact with the fabric into a thermal pressure system. Under the influence of the heat the dye sublimates and diffuses from the carrier into the fibre of the textile substrate. There is no need for further treatment such as steaming, washing, etc. This technique is applied for polyester; polyamide and some acrylic fibres, using selected disperse dyestuffs according to the specific type of fibre.

Fixation

After printing, the fabric is dried. Water evaporation leads to an increase in dye concentration and at the same time prevents the colours from smearing when the fabric is transported over the guide rollers. At this stage the dye is not yet fixed. The aim of the subsequent fixation step is to transport as much as possible of the dye, which is retained by the thickener, into the fibres. This is especially important with dyes, such as vat dyes, for example, that are printed in the insoluble form and are converted into the corresponding soluble state only after reaction with the reducing agents during the fixation process.

Fixation is usually carried out with steam. Water vapour condenses on the printed material, swells up the thickener, heats the print and provides the necessary transport medium for the diffusion of the dye. The distribution of the dye between fibre and thickener is an important factor in determining the fixation degree of the dye, which is called the "retaining power" of the thickener. The thickener, in fact, is often composed of polysaccharides and therefore competes with cellulose in retaining the dye. This is the main reason why the fixation rate of a given dye is 10 per cent lower in printing than in dyeing.

After-treatment

The last step of the printing process consists in washing and drying the fabric. When printing with insoluble dyes such as vat dyes this operation also serves as a means to re-convert the dye to the original oxidised state. In this case, after an initial rinsing with cold water, the printed material is treated with hydrogen peroxide. The process is completed with a soap treatment with sodium carbonate at the boiling point.

As already explained, washing is not necessary with pigment printing and transfer printing. This holds for any dyeing/printing system where thickeners are not needed and where the dyestuff is (nearly) completely fixed (*e.g.* printing carpet tiles with digital jet printing techniques).

Ancillary Operations

At the end of each batch and at each colour change various cleaning operations are carried out:

☆ The rubber belt, to which the fabric is glued during printing (see description below), is cleaned in continuous mode with water to remove excess adhesive and printing paste. Some machines are equipped with water re-circulation systems.

☆ The printing gears (all systems responsible for feeding and applying the paste to the substrate) are cleaned by first removing as much as possible of the paste residues and then rinsing with water. In some companies the paste residues are directed back to the appropriate printing paste batch containers for re-use.

☆ The remaining paste in the containers, in which the paste is prepared (paste vats), are in general previously cleaned up by means of sucking systems before being washed out with water. The residual printing paste collected in this manner is then disposed of.

Printing Technology

A variety of different machines can be used for printing fabrics. The most commonly used are described below.

Flat-Screen Printing

Flat-screen and rotary-screen printing are both characterised by the fact that the printing paste is transferred to the fabric through openings in specially designed screens. The openings on each screen correspond to a pattern and when the printing paste is forced through by means of a squeegee, the desired pattern is reproduced on the fabric. The method of screen printing with automatic squeegee system is shown in Figure 8.3. A separate screen is made for each colour in the pattern.

Flat-screen printing machines can be manual, semi-automatic or completely automatic. One type of machine, which is still commonly found in printing houses, is shown in Figures 8.4 and 8.5.

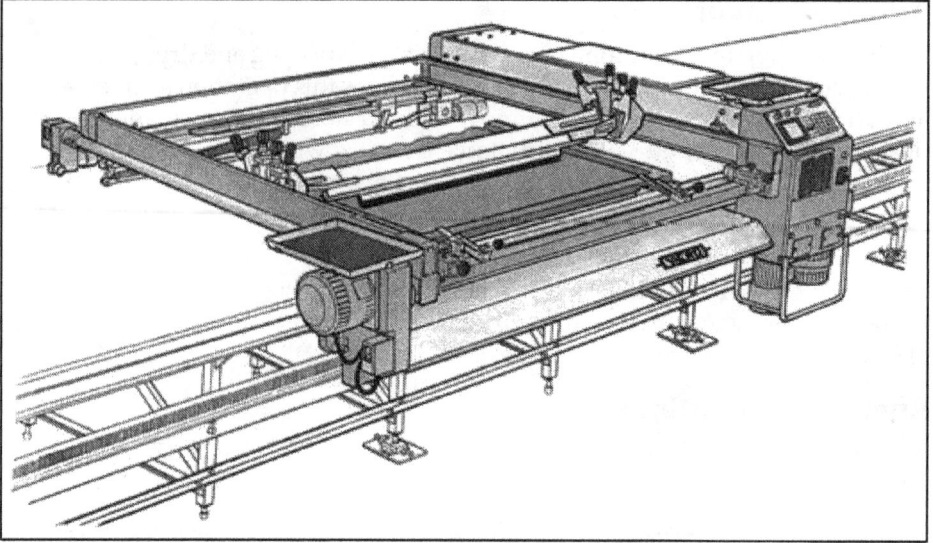

Figure 8.3: Screen Printing with Automatic Squeegee System.

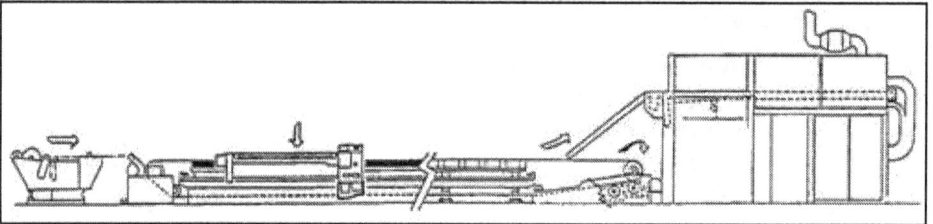

Figure 8.4: Representation of a Flat-Screen Printing Machine.

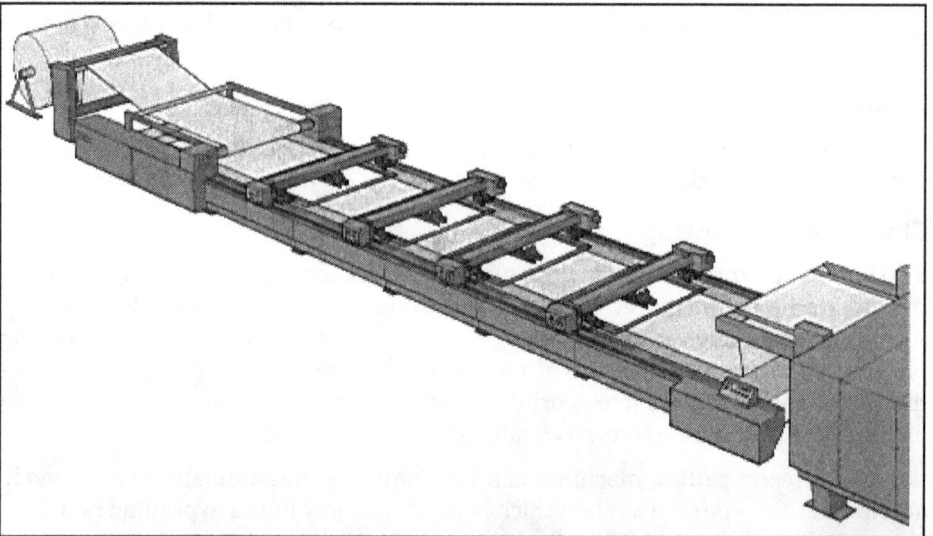

Figure 8.5: Representation of "Mechanised Screen Printing Machine with Stationary Screens Mounted in a Frame."

The fabric is first glued to a moving endless belt. A stationary screen at the front of the machine is lowered onto the area that has to be printed and the printing paste is wiped with a squeegee. Afterwards the belt, with the fabric glued on it, is advanced to the pattern-repeat point and the screen is lowered again. The printed fabric moves forward step by step and passes through a dryer. The machine prints only one colour at a time. When the first colour is printed on the whole length of the fabric, the dried fabric is ready for the second cycle and so on until the pattern is completed. In other fully mechanized machines all the colours are printed at the same time. A number of stationary screens (from 8 to 12, but some machines are equipped with up to 24 different screens) are placed along the printing machine. The screens are simultaneously lifted, while the textile, which is glued to a moving endless rubber belt, is advanced to the pattern-repeat point. Then the screens are lowered again and the paste is squeezed through the screens onto the fabric. The printed material moves forward one frame at each application and as it leaves the last frame it is finally dried and it is ready for fixation.

In both machines the continuous rubber belt, after pulling away the fabric, is moved downward in continuous mode over a guide roller and washed with water and rotating brushes to remove the printing paste residues and the glue, if necessary. After this, the belt is sent back to the gluing device. In some cases the glue is applied in liquid form by a squeegee, while in other machines the belts are pre-coated with thermoplastic glues. In this case the textile is heated and then it is squeezed by a roller or simply pressed against the rubber-coated belt, causing the glue to soften and instantly adhere. After printing, the screens and the application system are washed out. It is common practice to squeeze the colour from the screens back into the printing paste mixing containers before washing them.

Figure 8.6: Representation of the Rotary-Screen Printing Process.

Rotary-screen Printing

The rotary screen printing process is shown in Figure 8.6. Rotary-screen printing machines use the same principle described earlier, but instead of flat screens, the colour is transferred to the fabric through lightweight metal foil screens, which are made in the form of cylinder rollers. The fabric moves along in continuous mode under a set of cylinder screens while at each position the print paste is automatically fed to the inside of the screen from a tank and is then pressed through onto the fabric. A separate cylinder roller is required for each colour in the design. The rotary screen printing machine is shown in Figure 8.7.

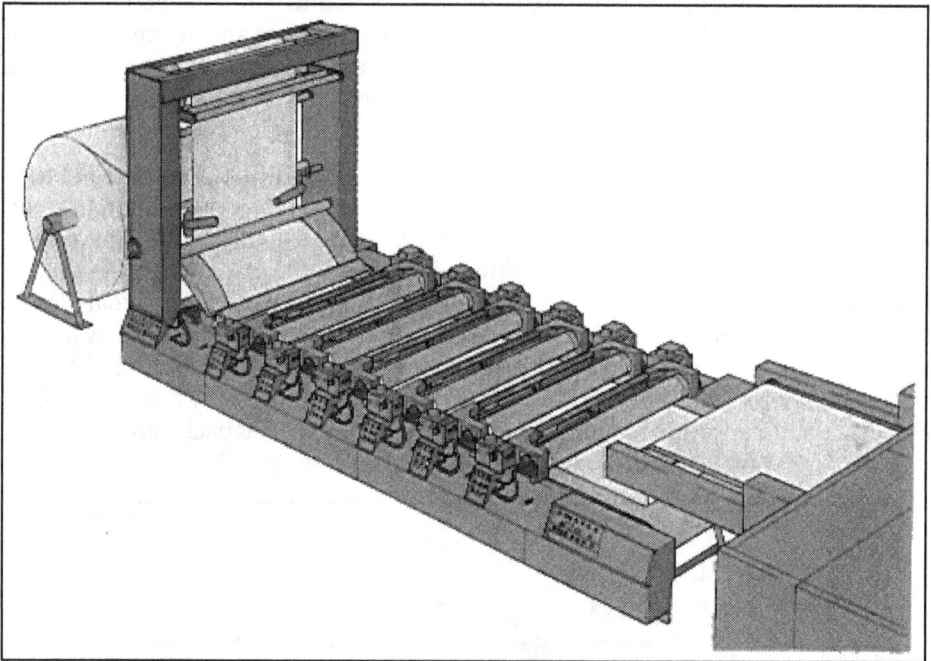

Figure 8.7: Representation of a Rotary-Screen Printing Machine.

A conventional paste feeding system for rotary-screen printing machines is represented below. A suction pipe leads from the paste vat to a pump, from where a printing hose leads to the squeegee (dye pipe with squeegee). From here the paste is directed inside the cylinder roller. The fill volume of this so-called printing paste input system is quite high and as a consequence the amount of paste residue that has to be removed at each colour change is also fairly significant. Various systems have been introduced in order to lower the volume configuration of this equipment, which also reduces the amount of such wastes. Another possibility, which has also already been implemented in some companies, is to recover and re-use these residues for making up new recipes.

The printing-paste feeding system for a rotary-screen printing machine is shown in Figure 8.8. Rotary-screen printing machines are equipped with both gluing and washing devices analogous to those described earlier for flat-screen printing. The belt is washed in order to remove the residues of paste and adhesive. Not only the belt, but also the screens and the paste input systems (hoses, pipes, pumps, squeegees, etc.) have to be cleaned up at each colour change.

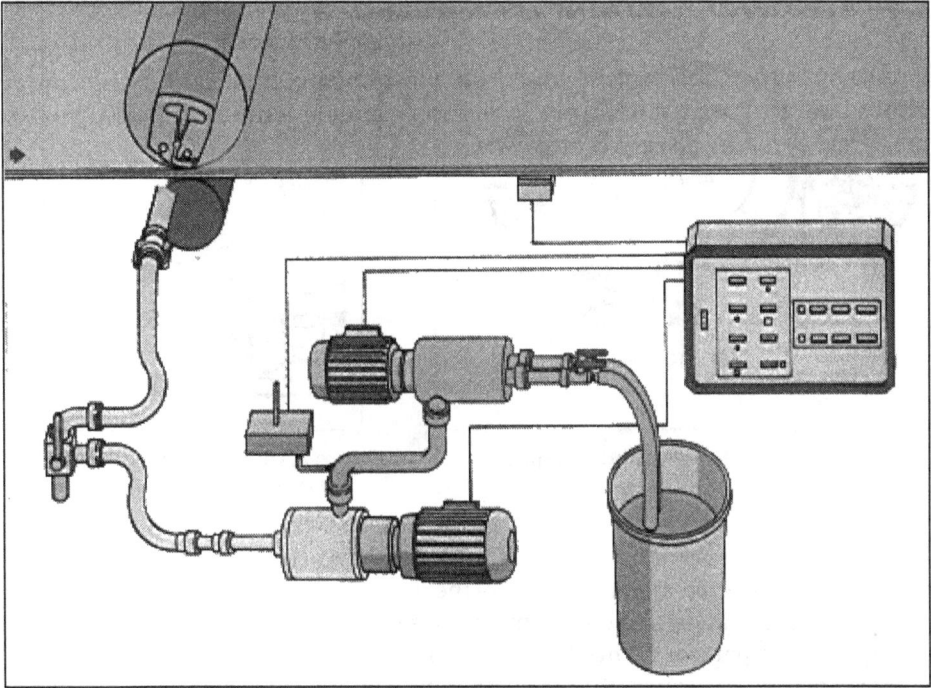

Figure 8.8: Printing-Paste Feeding System for a Rotary-Screen Printing Machine.

Roller Printing

The simple arrangement in roller printing machine is shown in Figure 8.9. In roller printing, the print paste is supplied from reservoirs to rotating copper rollers, which are engraved with the desired design. These rollers contact a main cylinder roller that transports the fabric. By contacting the rollers and the fabric the design is transferred to the fabric. As many as 16 rollers can be available per print machine; each roller imprints one repeat of the design. As the roller spins, a doctor blade in continuous mode scrapes the excess of paste back to the colour trough. At the end of each batch the paste reservoirs are manually emptied into appropriate printing paste batch containers and squeezed out. The belt and the printing gear (roller brushes or doctor blades, squeegees and ladles) are cleaned up with water. The more recent example of roller printing machine is shown in Figure 8.10.

Jet Printing

Jet printing is a non-contact application system originally developed for printing carpets, but now increasingly used in the textile sector. The first commercial jet printing machine for carpets was the Elektrocolour, followed by the first Millitron machine.

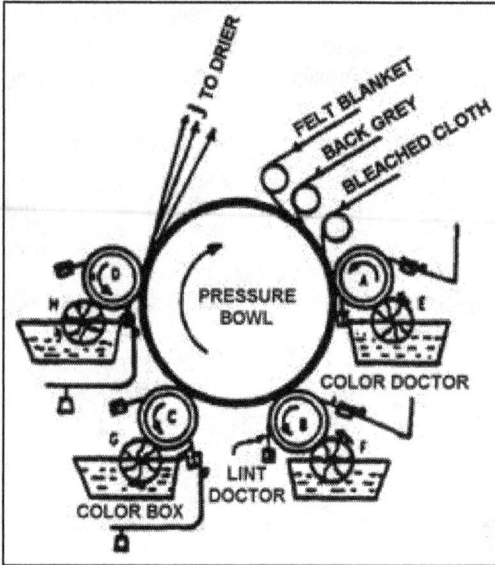

Figure 8.9: Roller Printing Machine.

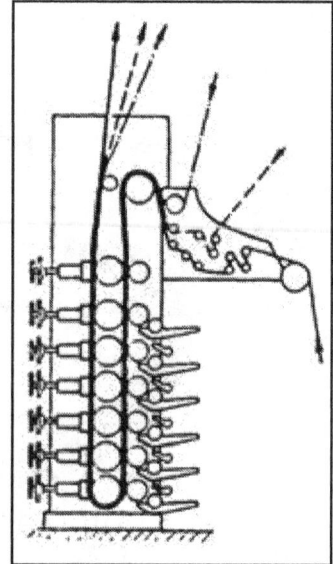

Figure 8.10: More Recent Example of Roller Printing Machine.

The Schematic representation of the Millitron system is shown in Figure 8.11. In the Millitron printing system, the injection of the dye into the substrate is accomplished by switching on and off a dye jet by means of a controlled air stream. As the carpet moves along, no parts of the machine are in contact with the face of the substrate. Air streams are used to keep continuously flowing dye jets, deflected into a catcher or drain tray. This dye is drained back to the surge tank, filtered and re-circulated. When a jet is requested to fire, the air jet is momentarily switched off, allowing the correct amount of dye to be injected into the textile substrate. The dye is supplied in continuous mode to the main storage tank to compensate for the amount of dye consumed.

Spray printing systems and first generation jet printing methods cannot be controlled to produce a pre-specified pattern. Thus the equipment must first be employed to produce a wide range of effects and only then can selections be made from these by the designer or marketing staff. An early improvement was made by the first digital carpet printers (Chromotronic and Titan by Zimmer and Tybar Engineering, respectively). These machines are based on the so-called «drop on demand principle», namely the use of switchable electromagnetic valves placed in the dye liquor feed tubes to allow the jetting of discrete drops of dye liquor in a predetermined sequence according to the desired pattern. In these machines, although the amount of dye applied can be digitally controlled at each point of the substrate, further penetration of the dye into the substrate is still dependent on capillary action of the fibre and fibre surface wetting forces. This can lead to problems of reproducibility (*e.g.* when the substrate is too wet) and means that it is still necessary to use thickeners to control the rheology of the dye liquor. The latest improvement in jet printing of

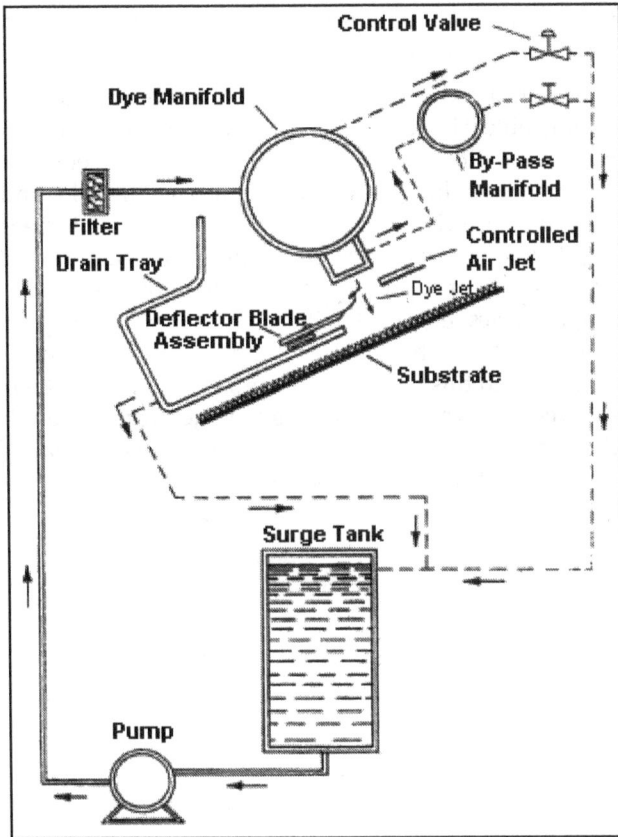

Figure 8.11: Schematic Representation of the Millitron System.

carpet and bulky fabrics is now represented by machines in which the colour is injected with surgical precision deep into the face of the fabric without any machine parts touching the substrate. Here, the control of the quantity of liquor applied to the substrate (which may vary for example from lightweight articles to heavy quality fabrics) is achieved by varying not only the firing time but also the pumping pressure.

This system can be likened to an injection dyeing process. The name (injection dyeing) is used as a commercial name to define the technology applied on the latest Milliken's Millitron machine. Another digital jet printing machine commercially available is Zimmer's Chromojet. In the Chromojet system, the

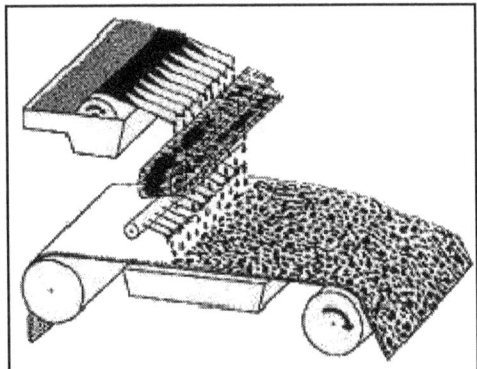

Figure 8.12: Schematic Representation of the TAK System.

printing head is equipped with 512 nozzles. These are magnetically controlled and can open and close up to 400 times a second.

The carpet is accumulated into a J-box, and is then steamed and brushed. When it reaches the printing table it is stopped. The jets are mounted on a sliding frame that can itself be moved in the direction of the warp while the carpet remains stationary during the printing process. Ink-jet printing is another digital printing technique with its origins in paper printing technology that is now also increasingly used in the textile industry. In ink-jet printing, colour is applied to the surface of the substrate without variation in firing time, pressure or velocity. For this reason it can only be applied for flat light fabrics, especially silk. The TAK printing system can still be found in the carpet industry. The Schematic representation of the TAK system is shown in Figure 8.12. With this technique irregular patterns can be produced. The carpet, previously dyed with a ground shade, is provided with coloured spots through dripping. The size and the frequency of the coloured spots can be varied by adjusting the overflow groove placed along the carpet width.

9

Traditional and Conventional Prints

Clothing and textiles have been important in human history and reflects the materials available to a civilization as well as the technologies that it has mastered. The social significance of the finished product reflects their culture. India is a country with rich tradition and religion which is reflected in the expression of folk art. The wearing of clothing is exclusively a human characteristic and is a feature of most human societies. It is not known when humans began wearing clothes. Alternatively, covering may have been invented first for other purposes, such as magic, decoration, cult, or prestige, and later found to be practical as well. Due to diversified talents, interests and inspiration, each state has its special identity for its unique creatures.

Kalamkari

The industry of dyeing and printing with local vegetable colours are known as "Kalamkari" work. Kalamkari work is being carried on at Machilipatnam from time immemorial. The printed cotton fabrics are of three types:

☆ Block Printed
☆ Block printed and Hand painted
☆ Hand painted only.

The graceful Kalamkari designs are symbols of skillful, talented craftsmen, who design them. Block making plays a crucial role, in printing a Kalamkari fabric, as it needs to be sharp. If the block is not good, the colours may spread around the cloth. The craftsmen who make these blocks take utmost care in carving them. Generally teak wood is used for engraving blocks. The wood selected should have no holes and cracks, and surface of the block is evened. The design to be carved is outlined on a paper sheet, which is stretched out evenly on the wood and gently tacked into place along the edges. A metal instrument, shaped like a pencil the sharp pointed edge, is lightly hammered along the lines of the pattern. This causes the transfer of the outline on to the wooden surface, and the block maker begins to etch the design. Although Kalamkari is practiced in other areas such as Kalahasti, the degree of commercialization and marketing linkages are in much greater evidence at Machilipatnam.

The kalamkari block printing produces a variety of designs on bed sheets, wall hangings, sarees, lungis, napkins etc. Many Islamic patterns are prominent among the designs of Machilipatnam. The designs produced are of three types, which are evolved to suit the needs of its consumers. The shamiyana covers and prayer cloth are painted with typical Persian designs, which are known as Gulabadami, Gulahati, Cherangmorkmath, Gulbechadar Bagal, Jaimaaz etc. Some of the products intended for export to western countries, are *Palang Posh* (bed sheets), door curtains, and tablecloth. Flowers, bird, and animal forms are the commonly used designs.

Designs are first outlined and then filled in by colour blocks. Only the indigenous colours are used. Sarees, door curtains, bed spreads are made with this design. Kalamkari is the most ancient industry in India. Sri Kalahasti in A.P is famous for Kalamkari hand printing. They are exclusively hand printed to be used as tapestries and hangings in temples. Here, vegetable dyes of deep rich shades are used with strong outlines in brown and black. All of which produced a bold and striking effect. Flowing water as from a river is desirable to clear it of starch as no washing material is used. It is next given a myrobelum solution bath to make black dye permanent. The Outlines of the drawing are traced out by free hand from memory or copied from an old piece with charcoal sticks made from tamarind twig. The final lines of the picture are drawn with a sharply pointed bamboo stick using Kalam, a mixture of molasses and iron filings. The artist first fills in the background colours, then the various figures, where red is the background. It is made a deeper shade by first applying alum to the cloth surface. The areas not covered by red, though faintly tinted can be bleached by the use of alum to enable them to take on other colours like blue, yellow, green.

Techniques of Kalamkari

Take camel or buffalo or cow dung equal to one fourth the weight of the grey and mix it with water. Dip grey cloth in mixture and leave for twelve hours. Then remove the cloth and wash it in running water and spread the cloth on green grass at the banks of the canal. Go on sprinkling water on the cloth as and when it gets dried till evening. As the sun rays fall on the cloth gradually it gets bleached. Repeat the process for three more days by which time it gets fully bleached. Finally wash the cloth in water and dry.

Application of Myrobelums

Take 25-30 gms/ltr myrobelums. Soak them a night in water. Afterwards crush the myrobelums and extract the juice. Then treat the bleached cloth by hand and dry. Now the cloth is ready for printing.

Preparation of Black Colour Solution

Black colour solution is prepared with iron pieces, old jaggery and well water. Take iron pieces, old jaggery and water in 2:1:10 ratios respectively. First burn the iron pieces. After getting cold clean the pieces of bricks and then wash well. Powder the old jaggery. Keep iron pieces and old jaggery powder in an earthen wear pot and pour well water. Close the lid. Open the lid weekly once and mix the solution by hand. After three weeks take out the iron pieces and use the black colour dye for printing. Used iron pieces can be reused for the preparation of black colour solution.

Block Printing

Prepare the black colour paste by taking black colour solution and gum Arabica crystals in 1:1 ratio. Print outlines with black colour paste. After completing the printing outlines with black, print alum (patika) paste was applied wherever the red colour is required. For preparing the alum paste take one kg of alum and boil for 30-45 min in about 5 liters of water. After boiling, about 2.5 litres of alum solution is obtained. Mix 2.5 kgs of the gum Arabica paste in the solution and use for printing. If the brown colour is required mix the black colour paste and alum paste in the ratio as per the requirement of the shade. After completing printing, dry the cloth.

Washing

Wash the printed cloth in flowing water. Thorough washing should be done. While washing care should be taken to avoid the folding of the cloth. Otherwise there will be a possibility of formation of stains while developing. Then dry the cloth.

Developing

Use copper vessels for developing. Take 0.5 to 1 g/ltr aliyerrine and prepare the solution with boiling water. Take water for developing at material to liquor ratio 1:20. Add the solution to the developing bath. Add jaji leaves to obtain uniform ground. Dip the above in the bath at 40°C and work. Raise the temperature gradually to boil with in one hour while turning the cloth in the developing bath. Red colour develops at the portions wherever the alum is printed and brown colour develops wherever the mixture black and alum is printed, then the cloth is washed and dried.

Application of Yellow Colour

For preparing yellow colour take 1kg of myrobalanm flowers and boil in about 5 litres of water. Boiling should be carried till the flower becomes soft. Then cool it and filter the solution. Paint with "kalam" on the starch applied cloth wherever the yellow colour is required.

Afterwards treat the cloth in 20 g/lt alum solution for about 10 min., which helps to fix the yellow colour on the cloth. Finally wash the cloth and dry. If white ground is required, again bleach the cloth with buffalo dung solution as explained above.

Normally the colours black, brown, red and yellow are used in kalamkari. Traditional method of application of indigo blue is not being followed by the printers as it is very time consuming and laborious. However vegetable indigo blue can be printed or painted by a vins caustic or hydrose. Take vegetable indigo blue cake, caustic, hydrose in 1:1:1 ratio, paste the indigo blue powder with little Turkey red oil and add required amount of water of 60°C temperature followed by the addition of caustic, mix well and add slowly hydrose by stirring the solution. Allow for 15 min for ageing. If it is for printings add gum arabica paste. If it is to be painted take directly for painting with brush on the starch applied cloth. After painting/printing dry the cloth and wash well in water. Green colour can be obtained by painting blue on yellow.

Growth of Dress out of Painting, Cutting

India is a country with rich tradition and religion which is reflected in the expression of folk art. Due to diversified talents, interests and inspiration, each state has its special identity for its unique folk painting. The art of madhubani painting is the traditional style developed in the surrounding villages of madhubani in Mithila region, Bihar. Madhubani is solely done by the women of the region; though today men are also involved to meet the demand. The work is done on freshly plastered or a mud wall.

For commercial purposes, the work is now being done on paper and cloth etc. The paintings are basically of a religious nature. They appear in the special rooms in their homes (in the pooja room, ritual area and bridal room) and on the main village walls, etc. for ceremonial or ritualistic purpose. Figures from nature and mythology are adopted to suit their style. Cotton wrapped around a bamboo stick are used as brush. The colours applied are prepared by the artists. The skill is handed down through generations, and hence the traditional designs and patterns are widely maintained.

Significance of Madhubani Wall Painting

Madhubani painting is a traditional folk art of region of Bihar. Madhubani means a "Forest of Honey", it is a place near Durbhanga district in North Bihar. So under this Mithilanchal region, these places famous for their beautiful traditional folk arts, which are named after this place and called Madhubani painting. The paintings on the wall have deeper themes and narratives as they are the stories told sometimes in a series of panels. Apart from their decorative purpose, they also constitute a form of visual education like picture books from which one learns about ones heritage. Some outstanding things are done in the Madubani area. They have naiveté and simplicity, which perhaps, attracts, soothes, pleases the eyes.

As Lord Ramah in wedding procession entered Mithila, this spectacle mythological tales and the flora and fauna of Mithila came alive as the wall decorations show. These beautiful expressions of human talents, carried down through tradition and custom are till today related to wedding decorations and bridal paraphernalia. This form of art is commonly known today as "Madhubani painting", after village in the Durbhanga district in Bihar where almost every home is decorated with painting made for ceremonial occasions.

Paintings on the wall are communal act done by all the women of a family or Group of women as part of rituals and festivals. The themes were taken from native Mythology, legends and history. This region has been swept of many religious emotions, including Buddhist and Tantric each leaving its own imprint through motifs in this place in the forms of picturisation. It's an important part of their religious thoughts. In their Ritual, the aspirations of the people to have the connection with the gods become a Vague sense of connection with the supreme god from whom men and women are separated.

The mythical stories of the heroes and heroines of the epics "Ramayana" and "Mahabharata" were also inherited by the folk; the Madhubani, through the recitation of these epic stories during the yearly festivals.

Colour Used for Painting

Colour of painting is used according to religious symbolism. Initially all vegetable dyes were used for the painting but today they have accessed to the variety of poster colours used according to their needs and to enable them for more experiments with colours. These paints have a narrow range of colours; generally Gulabi (Pink), Peela (Yellow), Neela (Blue), Sindhoora (Red) and suga Pankhi (Parrot Green). But colours used in Madhubani paintings are usually deep red, green, blue, black etc. Besides deep colour they also apply light yellow, pink and lemon.

Brush Used for Painting

A suitable surface on the wall, the requisite paints and finally, some brushes are required for painting. When the paints are ready, the artists apply two kinds of country brushes, neither of which has yet been commercialized. For outlines and tiny details a small bamboo twig is used, its end being slightly frayed, so that the fibre is like hair, while for putting on the larger washes a small piece of cloth is tied to a twig, popularly known as *"Pihua"*. The women with very limited resources use indigenous colours that they can make themselves and finally bamboo sticks wrapped in cotton used for painting.

Material Used for Painting

As this tradition was initialized with a purpose of decorating the exterior of the house, the walls and the floors are always served as the canvas. To bring the maximum effect the walls and floor of the house was coated with cow dung and mud paste. When it dried it will give a perfect dark background to the bright painting done with white rice paste. Later they were noticed by the urban people and the art moved to hand made papers as the painted walls could not be moved to their living rooms.

Symbols Used in Madhubani Painting

The highly symbolic paintings were used "Khobargas" (Bridal Chambora) where couples spent the first few days of the married life. Here there will be divine couples like Shiva-Parvati, Radha-Krishna.

☆ **Animal Forms:** There are images of birds and animals with natural phenomena. Then sign of fertility and prosperity for good luck like elephant, fishes, tortoise, parrots, peacocks etc.

☆ **Human Forms:** In this paintings include various Gods and Goddesses. The subject matter varies according to the occasion.

☆ **Other Forms:** In other forms, the flora, fauna, myth and legend, social customs m and expressions giving ritualistic symbols are painted. In these paintings include flower (Lotus tree, bamboo forest etc.)

Tie and Dye

Style of Dyed and Printed Textile of India

Tie dyeing is one of the techniques of decorating fabric. The technology is based on resist dyeing and the resisting material used is thread. The fabric is tied tightly with string so that when it is put into the dye bath, the colour cannot penetrate the parts tied. When opened out, this leaves a pattern on a coloured background. This technology is much suitable to the rural women as it can provide livelihood for them. It can ensure sustainable income to the rural families as there is great demand for these dyed and printed textiles.

Tools and Accessories Required

Basins, Bowls, Stove, Large wooden spoons, white thread (Sewing thread), Dyes, Fabric, etc.

Suitable Fabrics for Tie and Dye

Georgette, Lawn, Cambric, Poplin, Silk, Mulmul, Voile etc. Light weight fabrics are easiest as they take up the dye quickly, but heavier fabrics can also be used if they are left longer in the dye bath.

Preparation of Materials

Both new as well as used material can be given a new looking by means of applying fresh colours and design. In the case of new materials the starch or sizing present should be removed thoroughly. Further, soak the material in cold water for 6-8 hours. Then rinse in fresh water several times, dry the fabric and press it flat.

Thin materials namely georgette or mulmul may be tied after folding to minimize the work. First fold length wise into half and then width wise into half. Now the fabric is in four layers. The fabric should not have more than four layers. In case of thick fabrics the material should not be folded at all. The design must be tied at a time on all the layers of the fabric.

Techniques of Tie and Dye

Knotting

It is the simplest method of producing tie and dye designs. This produces some what circular hazy patterns without the use of any tieing material. Pick up the fabric at a point and make a firm knot. When this technique is used on a square material make a big knot in the centre and make knots at the corners.

Tiny Dots

This is the most widely used technique and is popularly known as bandhani work. Pick up little fabric and tie around three to four times to produce tiny dots. These dots may be lined of scattered or outlined into the shape of a design. The thread is generally carried from one tie to the other to speed up the work. Metal blocks with raised portions as per the design may be employed for design transfer.

Objects Resist Tying

To get even doted patterns, tie objects of the same size and shape. Insert the objects into the fabric and tie around. To produce variety objects of different shapes and sizes can be introduced.

Pleating

Pleating and tieing the fabric produces the stripes of various styles. For a straight stripe pattern, fold the fabric into tiny pleats either horizontally or vertically as per the direction of the stripes. Tie at intervals. If wider stripers are required, tie the thread covering wider space. For diagonal stripes, pleat the fabric diagonally and tie. Tieing and dyeing in different colours produce multi colour stripes.

Bundling

Folding and bundling fabric produce wide variety of designs. Fold the fabric in various ways- horizontally, vertically or diagonally into a square or a rectangle or a triangle. Tie vertically, horizontally and also tie the corners for geometrical patterns.

Tritic

Tritic is a sewing technique suitable for producing more fine and sharp designs. Even though it is easier to produce geometrical designs, floral designs can also be achieved. Transfer the design onto the fabric and work running stitches with loose thread along the lines of the design. After all details of the design are stitched, pull each thread and draw the fabric tightly and then tie the thread firmly wrapping around and knotting. Stitches other than running stitch may be employed for producing various effects

Spider Web

This generally forms the centre pattern in a design and it resembles the spider web, hence the name. Pick up the centre point of the fabric and gather the fabric around into tiny folds, depending on the radius of the web required, tie the thread around the folds from top to the required depth. The direction of tying can be varied to produce various effects.

Marbling

Marbled effect is produced by holding the fabric in hand and crumpling into a ball and tying around securely. Care should be taken to expose the fabric from all sides, so that marbling is even. For getting multicoloured effect, the thread can be opened after one dyeing and again tied in the same way exposing the uncovered areas.

Dye Preparations and Methods of Dyeing

Naphthol Dyes

Naphthol dyes give brilliant colours to cotton and have a wide range of colours. Except green shades, other colours are possible using naphthol dyes. Generally naphthol dyes are used for producing yellows, oranges, reds and maroons.

Naphthol dyes has two components. Naphthol a coupling agent/or a developer and a diazotized salt or base. Naphthol and base are taken in equal quantities for most of the combinations. The dyed cottons show good fastness to washing and perspiration and also resist staining. But it looses colour through crocking and sunlight fading. Care should be taken not to dry the naphthol dyed cotton in sun and avoid rubbing during use. Naphthol is the developer and base is the dyestuff.

Method of Preparation

Take two vessels. In the first vessel mix Monopal soap with hot water and add the developer. Make a fine paste. To this add one cup of soft water and boil it for 10 minutes. Then add Caustic soda. Now this solution will become clear. Add cold soft water to make up to 2 lit and stir it well. Remove the fabric from steeping water. Press well to remove extra water. Open the fabric and immerse in naphthol solution, turn it up and down so that solution can be spread evenly. Leave the fabric in solution for 10 to 20 min.

In the mean time, take the second vessel and prepare the base solution (dye). Make a smooth paste of dye with little hot water. Add this to two litres of soft water and stir it well. Add HCl. Add sodium nitrite to complete diazotization. Now remove the fabric from naphthol solution and drench in the above solution for one hour. Turn the fabric up and down so that colour spreads evenly. To deepen the shade, wash the dyed fabric and enter into the naphthol solution and repeat the process.

After Treatment

Stoop the dyed material in hot detergent solution (2 gms soap or detergent/lit) to fix the dye and to remove the loose dye from the surface. It aids in better colour fastness properties.

Vat Dyes

Vat dyes are fast dyes for cotton. These dyes offer a range of light and dark shades. The popular shades include greens, browns, purples, and limited yellow shades etc. Vat dyes are originally insoluble in water. They are made soluble by the addition of caustic soda and sodium hydro sulphite. The dye is impregnated on fabric in a reduced state and then reoxidised again on fabric. Hence, the colours are fast and do not generally loose colour through washing, crocking, perspiration and sunlight. Two types of vat dyes are sold in the market. The hot colours are used for Tie and Dye. The cold colours are used for Batik.

Method of Preparation

Soak the desired fabric in cold water. Weigh the cloth to be dyed. Take the weighed dye and make it into smooth paste by adding Turkey red oil. Dilute the colour paste with measured quantity of water and add caustic to the diluted colour. Add measured amount of caustic and stir. Then add hydrose and observe the change of colour. Green colour changes to blue, yellow colour changes to violet etc. Then prepare the dye bath by adding water. The material liquor ratio should be 1:20 and then see the concentration of colour. If the colour changes back again to the original colour, sprinkle more hydrose till colour change is noticeable. This should be done in a closed vessel. Place this fabric in the dye bath for 20 minutes. Stir the liquid continuously. Then take out the material and wash it under running water. Oxidize the colour by frequent airing and washing or by using peroxide bleach. Soap the material, thoroughly as in naphthol dyeing to remove unfixed dye. Finally wash the material till the water becomes clear.

Dye Calculation

The dyestuff required to dye a material depends on the depth of shade required and weight of the fabric. If 2 per cent shade is required to dye 100 gms of fabric then multiply the weight of the fabric by the shade.

Amount of dyestuff = Weight of the fabric X per cent depth of shade.

Dye required = 100 g X 2/100 = 2 g.

Precautions

☆ Make dye paste with little cold or hot water. Never add more water while making the dye paste.

☆ Accurate weighing is required.

☆ Store dyes and chemicals in air tight bottles to preserve the potency.

☆ Use gloves while dyeing, some dyes and chemicals are harmful to the skin.

☆ Care must be taken while using acids.

☆ The platform and floor of the dyeing place should be protected from the dye stains.

☆ The fabric should be opened fully and immersed in dye bath. It should always be in immersed condition with continuous stirring.

☆ The temperature should be maintained.

☆ Rinsing should be done thoroughly to remove excess dye.

To obtain Three Colours namely White, Yellow and Red

☆ After tying some dots for white, immerse the fabric in yellow colour. Then tie for yellow dots. Now immerse in red colour. This will result in yellow and white dots with red back ground.

☆ White, yellow and green: First tie the dots on white fabric. Then dye it in yellow. Tie a few more areas to preserve yellow dots. To obtain a final background in green colour, dye in green colour.

☆ To obtain two colours namely white dots and coloured background: Tie the dots according to the pattern or design and dye in any suitable dye.

Opening the Thread of Tied Portion

If a continuous thread is used for tying of the dots, then the material should be pulled cross wise in order to open the tied portion. The fastened portion easily opens out when pulled. If the thread is cut after each dot or portion being tied, each knot should be removed or snipped separately. While snipping the thread, care must be taken to see that the material is not caught and cut.

Batik

Batik is a resist dyeing method and the resisting material used is wax. Pattern on material is made by painting the design on the fabric with very hot liquid wax on both sides, before immersing in dye bath. The wax prevents the dye reaching the painted pattern and finished material is left with pale pattern on a coloured background. The wax is sometimes deliberately cracked to form fine spider like line of colour where the dye penetrates through these cracks. The dye bath is always cold, otherwise the wax would melt.

Fabrics, Materials and Tools

The fabrics used for batik should be smooth and thin in order to get a good effect. Silk is perhaps the easiest fabric of all to use, fine lawn comes second. Heavy coarse and thick fabrics are not much used. Any fabric for making batik should be thoroughly washed and ironed before use. Cottons should be desized before. Dyes will not be absorbed properly if the fabric is not clean.

Wax

Bees wax is the best wax for batik for fine lines and small areas. This is rather expensive but more manageable and forms less cracks than other kinds. Rosin can be added in proportion of 1:4 of bees wax. Rosin is used if fewer cracks are required, but for design areas bees wax and paraffin are used.

Brushes

Brushes of various sizes will be needed to apply wax. Cheap brushes can be used for large areas and one or two good stable brushes should be kept for fine and delicate lines. Brushes should be rinsed well in petrol immediately after use, and then should be washed in warm water and soap and dried. The brushes made with long handle and pointed edge and ball of thread are handier to hold hot wax for a long time.

Tjanting and Tjap

Tjanting has a metal cup with a pointed spout and a wooden handle. Tjaps are metal blocks and the stamp face of the Tjap is immersed in hot melted wax.

Tracing the Design on the Fabric

The fabric must be ironed well and must be stretched firmly over a frame. Then the design is traced lightly on the fabric with a pointed pencil.

Application of Wax on the Cloth

Design in Single Colour

1. **Batik:** The design on the fabric is made by applying very hot liquid wax on both the sides, in the required areas of the design. The wax to be applied on cloth has to be hot so that the liquid penetrates through the cloth. The wax dries immediately as it is applied on the fabric. The wax prevents the dye penetrating into the design. After dyeing, the material is left with the patterns on a coloured background. It is also possible to get a reverse effect by applying wax on the background and leaving the pattern untouched.

2. **Multi-colour Design:** The multicolour design, parts of the design to be left white are waxed and dyed in the lightest colour. After it is dry, wax is applied on the portions of the design, which are to be retained in light colour. Then the fabric is dipped in the second dye bath which is brighter. Remove from dye bath and rinse well.

3. **Crackled Design:** This can be obtained by applying wax throughout the cloth on both the sides or dipping in hot wax. Then it is soaked in water and after taking out from water, crackles can be made by pressing between hands. After this, it is dyed. If crackles of two colours are desired, apply wax again on the dyed cloth on both sides and repeat the process to get the crackles by pressing the cloth by hands in opposite directions.

Dyeing Procedure

After applying wax, the fabric is immersed in cold water, before dyeing to ensure that the wax is hard and wet. This makes the fabric to absorb the dye easily. Dyeing procedure is as per the type of fabric chosen. Only cold dye methods are employed. When the dye bath is ready, the waxed material is taken out of cold water and squeezed well to crack the wax if necessary. It should be turned gently once or twice to ensure even dyeing and leaving in dye basin for 15 min to 30 min. rinse well and dry.

Removal of Wax from the Fabric

☆ When the fabric is dried after dyeing, the wax must be removed. Thick wax can be cracked off by working the fabric with hands. Then washed in petrol.

☆ Place the fabric in between two pieces of blotting papers or any paper and iron with a hot iron. The melted wax will be absorbed by the paper.

☆ The wax from cotton material can be removed by soaking in hot soap water with little caustic soda and little kerosene. Several hot soaping are required to make fabric free of wax. Rinse it well immediately with soap and water.

Methods of Printing

Colour designs are produced on fabrics by printing with dyes in paste form or by positioning dyes on the fabric from specially designed machines. One form of applying colour decoration to a fabric after it has otherwise been finished is called printing. Printed fabrics usually have clear-cut edges in the design portion on the right side and the colour seldom penetrates completely to the wrong side of the fabric. Yarns raveled from printed fabrics will have colour unevenly positioned on them.

Block Printing

Block printing is a hand process and the oldest technique for decorating textiles. It is seldom done commercially because it is costly and slow. A design is carved on a block. The block is dipped in a shallow pan of dye and stamped on the fabric. To obtain variation of colour in the same design, as many additional blocks must be carved as there will be additional colours. The more colours used the more valuable and expensive the block print will be. Slight irregularities in colour register or positioning are clues to block prints but these can be duplicated in roller printing made to resemble them.

Simple designs are suitable for block printing. Too many details in the design must be avoided. The number of colours should be kept to the minimum. Though these blocks can be made from potato, linoleum etc., wood is the most commonly used medium. The design is varied by scooping the wood so that it is either outstanding or is in relief. The number of blocks required for a design corresponds to number of colours in the design.

Materials for Printing

The materials required for printing are:

a) A table of convenient size which is covered with several layers of jute hessian cloth and a layer of grey cloth.

b) A few trolleys to carry dyes around the table.

c) A few trays made of enamel wood.

d) Thin sponge sheet

e) Hessian cloth, muslin and mosquito net cloth.

f) Wooden piece with a flat edge.

g) Mortar and pestle for making dye paste.

h) Containers for dye paste.

i) Facilities for drying, steaming and washing

Rapid Colours

Dye Proportion

Dye 12.5 g

Sodium Hydroxide 6.5 g

Warm Water 18c.c. or (1 part)

Urea 9 g

Neutral gum paste 125c.c.

Water to make up to 500c.c.

Turkey red oil few drops

Method

Prepare smooth paste of the dye with little warm water and Turkey red oil in a mortar. Add half of the gum to which little sodium hydroxide has already been added to neutralize it. Make a homogenous paste by mixing with the pestle. Then add the remaining NaOH solution and stir well. Add the remaining gum and urea and stir. Add water to make upto 500c.c. and to obtain a dye of desirable consistency. The fabric after printing should be dried in sunlight for one day. Some after treatment has to be given to fix the dye.

After Treatments

- ☆ **Sulphuric Acid:** The water to material ratio should be 20:1 in one litre of water 3-4 ml of sulphuric acid should be added. The material should be immersed in this solution for half an hour at room temperature and then washed with soap and water.

- ☆ **Steaming:** The printed material should be wrapped in news paper and steamed in a closed vessel for 10-20 minutes.

Screen Printing

Originally this technique was referred to as silk-screen printing because the screens were made of fine, strong silk threads. Today they are also made of nylon, polyester, and metal. *Flat screen printing* was done by hand. It is done commercially for small yardages, 50-5,000 yards, and is used extensively for designs larger than the circumference of the rolls used for roller printing. The design is applied to the screen so that all but the figure is covered by a resist material. One screen is used for each colour. The colour is forced through the screen by a squeegee. In the hand process, the fabric to be printed is placed on a long table. Two people position the screen on the fabric, apply the colour, move the screen to a new position, and repeat the process until all the fabric is printed.

In the automatic screen process, the fabric to be printed is placed on a conveyer belt. A series of flat screens are positioned above and are lowered automatically. Colour is applied automatically, and the fabric is moved automatically and fed continuously into ovens to be dried.

Rotary screen printing is done with cylindrical metal screens that operate in much the same way as the flat screens except that the operation is continuous rather than started and stopped as the screens are raised and lowered in the flat. The rotary screens are cheaper than the copper rollers used in roller printing. The chief advantages of screen printing are that the colours can be produced in brighter, cleaner shades than are possible with roller printing and the designs to be repeated can be much larger. It is possible to have designs consisting of squares, circles, and ovals. On a knitted fabric, such as jersey, flat and rotary screen printing the transfer printing are the only printing methods that can be used. Other methods smear dyes as a knitted fabric stretches when it receives the impact of the rollers.

Stencil Printing

This is originated in Japan. Its high cost, limits its use and importance. In the U.S., in stencil printing, the design must first be cut on cardboard, wood, or metal. The stencil may have a fine, delicate design or there may be large spaces through which a great amount of colour can be applied. A stencil design is usually limited to the application of only one colour and is generally used for narrow widths of fabric. Stencil printing is one of the methods of resist printing and the resisting material used is wax paper or stencil sheet. This can be used for printing design both on paper and cloth. The number of colours to be used on the design is same as the number of stencil sheets cut.

Design Suitable for Stencil Printing

Design for stenciling should consist of clear definite shapes. Fine lines and small details are to be avoided as they are difficult both to cut and to stencil.

Tools and Materials

1. Thick drawing papers for marking the stencils.
2. A stencil knife or a sharp blade.
3. Glass sheet as cutting surface.
4. Stencil brushes of various sizes, sponges, gun spray.
5. Paraffin wax.
6. Water colours for paper
7. Fabric paints.
8. Medium for paints.
9. Bundle of papers to provide backing.

Procedure

Choose a suitable design for a mono and multicolour scheme. A convenient design is one which the individual parts of the design are separate from each other.

Preparation of Stencil Sheets

Measure the size of the design and decide the colour scheme. Cut stencil cards separately for each colour. Prepare cards by cutting drawing paper 2" to 3" bigger than the size of the design. Transfer the design on to the cards leaving 1" to 1.5" border on all sides and taking care to transfer the design exactly in the same place in all cards. Mark the parts of the design to be cut for one colour in one card. Melt wax, dip the cards in wax and allow for dry. Lay the stencil on glass plate, cut smoothly along the parts of the design using a sharp stencil blade for achieving success. Cut the remaining cards separately for each colour. Hold all cards together against the light to check the accuracy of the design.

- ☆ **Printing:** Fabric paints are used for printing on fabrics and water colours can be used for printing on paper. For applying colour, stencil brushes, sponges, tooth brushes and gun sprays can be used.
- ☆ **Stencil Brushes:** Select brushes with soft bristles and blunt ends which preserve the stencil better. Use separate brush for each colour.
- ☆ **Tooth Brushes:** They give sprayed effect. The brush is held over the area to be coloured and then rubbed with the thumb.
- ☆ **Sponges:** These can be used with water colours and thinned acrylics to create soft, mottled effects. Cut a flat sponge into strips about one inch wide and dip one end into the colour.

Air Brush or Gun Spray

This special purpose tool is used for getting spray effect to colour large areas in limited time. Direct, acid or vat dyes dissolved in water, alcohol or other organic solvent may be used. Place a bundle of papers on the table to offer a soft backing while printing and place material to be printed over this and pin securely. Prepare the colour in a thick consistency on a palette. Try out the colour with the brush to see whether the colour is being transferred on the material evenly by working the brush first on the glass sheet, then on the paper. When colour is applied evenly, then the work can be started on the material. While dabbing the colour, the brush should be kept up right to get a sharp neat outline. For a multi colour design, the second colour is applied after the first one is partially dry.

Precautions

1. Never exert pressure on the brush while printing.
2. Never wet brushes.
3. Always dab up and down.

Roller Printing

Direct roller printing was developed in 1785, about the time all textiles operations were becoming mechanized. It turns out colour designed fabrics in vast quantities at the rate of 1000 to 4000 yards an hour. This method of producing attractive designs is relatively inexpensive when compared with any hand method. It is a machine counter part of block printing. Essential parts of the printing machine A cast-iron cylinder is the roller around which the cloth is drawn as it is printed. The copper printing roller is etched with the design.

Originally, the design was engraved by hand an awl; today, the engraving is frequently done pantograph transfer and by photoengraving. There are as many different rollers as there are colours in the fabric. In the diagram (Figure 8.9) three engraved rollers are used. Furnisher rollers are covered with hard rubber or brushes made of nylon, or hard-rubber bristles. They revolve in a small colour bath, pick up the colour, and deposit it on the copper rollers.

A doctor blade scrapes off excess colour so that only the engraved portions of the copper roller are filled with dye when it comes in contact with the cloth. The cloth to be printed, a rubberized blanket, and a back gray cloth pass between the cylinder and the engraved rollers. The blanket gives a good surface for sharp printing; the gray goods protect the blanket and absorb excess dye. Rayon and knitted fabrics are usually lightly coated with a gum sizing on the back to keep them from stretching or swelling as they go through the printing machine. After printing, the cloth is dried, steamed, or treated to set the dye.

Discharge Printing

Discharge prints are piece dyed fabrics in which the design is made by removing the colour. Discharge prints are usually done on dark backgrounds. A discharge paste, which contains chemicals to remove the colour, is then printed on the fabric. Dyes that are not harmed by the discharging materials can be mixed with printing solution if colour is desired in the discharge areas. The fabric is then steamed to develop design, either as a white or coloured area. Discharge prints can be detected by looking at the wrong side of the fabric. In the design area the colour is often not completely removed and one can see evidences of the background colours, especially around the edges of the design. Background colours must be colours that can be removed by strong alkali. Discharge prints are usually satisfactory.

Bandhani

Bandhanis or choonaris are the colourful sari and odhnis dyed by tie and dye process. These are popular amongst the women of Gujarat, Kathaiwar, Rajasthan and Sindh. Indian women are known for their love for bright colours. Also the tradition and the customs of wearing special colours on different festivals, makes it necessary for them to become familiar with the art of dyeing at home. Thus besides the expert professional dyers almost every Indian girl learns by practice a good deal of the art of dyeing and Bandhani work.

Bandhani differ from Patola as regards the stage at which they are dyed. Like Patolas they are dyed by the tie and dye process, which, however, is done after the fabric is woven. The fabric is folded over several times until reduced to a small thick square or a rectangular piece. The piece is then damped and pressed on a block on which a design is carved. The impressed portions are picked up by the finger nails (the nails are allowed to grow especially for the purpose and are used as a sort of pincers) and are then tied up with cotton thread in a thickness sufficient to resist the dye. It needs training and great skill to pick up all the layers at once and make it crinkle in a particular given manner. The bandhanari or the woman who does the tying up work, works swiftly and ties up all the impressed portions without cutting the thread but carries it over from one point to the next. The dyeing process is carried out in the same order as in Patolas, starting with the light colours and finishing with the dark ones. But each time, before a new shade colour is applied the tieing up process has got to be repeated. Usually, the designs used are copies of a few traditional ones and by the practice of tieing up the same design over and over again the bandhanaris become expert to such an extent that they are able to dispense with the process of impressing the fabric with the design. The motifs of the traditional designs used for Bandhanis represent animals, birds, flowers and dancing dolls. When elaborate designs are used the Bandhanis are known as "Gharchola". In some of the expensive "Gharchola" gold threads are woven in to form checks or squares, and then the designs are formed in each of the squares by the tie and dyed process. The "Choonaris" are very light fabrics, and the designs for these consist of dots or pin heads irregularly spread all over the field of the cloth. Sometimes the dots are grouped together to form a design, and the design is known as "Ek bundi" (one dot), "Char bundi" (four dots) and "Sat bundi" (seven dots).

Patola

It was among the choicest exports from the great textile centre in Surat along the Caravan routes to the markets of Samarkhand, Bohkhara, Baghdad, Basra, Damascus and Rome in the 15th and 16th Centuries. The making of a Patola is a difficult and complicated process. Its unique quality is that the threads of the warp and weft are separately dyed in portions in such a way that the patterns on the finished product emerge in weaving. Patola manufacturer is restricted now-a-days but a few rare, choice pieces are still available. A type of Patola technique is employed in other parts of India to produce saris, bedspreads curtains and a variety of other fabrics.

Patola or Ikkat Fabrics

The Ahmedabad Patola is a textile of a unique character. Mahesana district, in Ahmedabad is noted for the beautiful material. The methods of weaving in the ikkats of Orissa, the Pochampalli textiles and the Patola are some what similar, but the Patola weaver has retained his geometric designs. Whatever patterns or floral motifs he may choose for his materials he prefers to set them in geometric order. The order in the development of artistic work has always shown that geometric patterns coming the earlier stages, while stylized and floral motifs follow later. We may thus conclude that the ikkats are the later innovations of the Patola style of weaving. The riot of colour in the Patola makes it gorgeous. The interesting point in these textiles is the fact that the yarn in the warp is first dyed or block printed. according to the requirement of the motif. The design is achieved in the fabric almost with miraculous effect with a simple operation of the wool. One of the loveliest contributions of the Indian dyer's skill to the world of textiles is the Patola, a kind of double ikkats where in the warp and weft threads are first tie-dyed and subsequently woven together, the dyed areas of the fibres coming together wonderfully to form the desired designs. The Patola technique is seen at its best in the silk wedding saris of Gujarat and Kathaiwar. The warp and the weft threads are separately dyed by the bandhani process. The silk warp is first dyed in the lightest colour and the dyer, keeping in mind the design to be produced.

10

Finishing

Value Addition is the process where we enhance the salability of the product by adding some incentives to it. Gone are the days when quality product was the only criterion to eye a product by a consumer. Earlier were the times when sheer competitiveness in the domestic market was very confined. But, during some part years with the emergence of globalization, competitive atmosphere and quality consciousness, has reached a new mark. With the steady improvement in technology and application standards, a gradual rise was observed in consumer demands. And to reach up to that mark, manufacturers have to add something to their products to get some added value for their products.

Antimicrobial Finishes

Among the various antimicrobial agents used for the finishing of textile substrates, silver or silver ions have long been known to have strong inhibitory and bacterial effects as well as a broad spectrum of antimicrobial activities. The inhibitory effect of silver ion/silver metal on bacteria has been attributed to the interaction of silver ion with thiol groups in bacteria as well as to the oxidative destruction of microorganism in aqueous medium. Silver ion based antimicrobial finishes have been developed by the interaction of a silver salt such as silver nitrate with anionic copolymer of styrene, ethyl acrylate, acrylic acid and divinyl benzene having at least about 0.008 molar equivalent of carboxyl groups per gram of polymer and ^{3} 0.0009 m mol of silver per gram of the polymer. The films of such polymeric finishes release antibacterial and anti fungal silver ions slowly over a very long period of time. In another patent, it is disclosed that a silver containing antimicrobial agent that has affinity for textile fibres can be produced by treating cross-linked carboxy methyl cellulose (CMC) having

> 0.4 carboxy methyl groups with silver nitrate. The antimicrobial finishing agent may have 0.01 - 0.1 per cent silver bound to the water resistant cross-linked CMC (Ag).

Odour Fights Finish

A Taiwanesse nanotech firm Greensheild has created underwear that fights odour. This is achieved through nanotechnolgy. The underwear fibres release undetectable negative ions and infrared rays that destroy odour-causing bacteria. The negative ions create a magnetic field that inhibits the reproduction of bacteria, thus eliminating odour and lowering the risk of skin infection or irritation. Far infrared rays are absorbed by cells not just in the skin but throughout the body – causing all the individual atoms being vibrated at a higher frequency, which speeds up the metabolism and the elimination of wastes. Tourmaline a natural mineral limits a low-level radiation which in contact with oxygen, carbon dioxide and water molecules in the air promotes electrolytic dissociation and emits negative ions. This Nano finish can eliminate up to 99.99 per cent of bacteria, 90 per cent of odour and 75 per cent sticky moisture within the cloth as well as contributing to the overall health of wearer.

Anti-Static Finish

Static charge usually formed during processing synthetic fibres such as nylon and polyester because of their moisture content. Cellulose fibre such as cotton has higher moisture content to carry away static charges, so that no static charge will accumulate. But the synthetic fibres provide poor anti-static properties. It was determined that nano-sized titanium dioxide, zinc oxide whiskers, nano antimony-doped tin oxide (ATO) and silane nanosol could impart anti-static properties to synthetic fibres. TiO_2, ZnO and ATO provide anti-static effects because they are electrically conductive materials. Such material helps to effectively dissipate the static charge which is accumulated on the fabric. On the other hand, silane nanosol improves anti-static properties, as the silane gel particles on fibre absorb water and moisture in the air by amino and hydroxyl groups and bound water.

UV-Protection

Previously organic and inorganic UV absorbers were coated on the textile material they prevent UV radiation effectively but they are less durable. UV blockers are usually certain semiconductor oxides such as TiO_2, ZnO, SiO_2 and Al_2O_3. Among these semiconductor oxides, titanium dioxide (TiO_2) and zinc oxide (ZnO) are commonly used. It was determined that nano-sized titanium dioxide and zinc oxide were more efficient at absorbing and scattering UV radiation than the conventional size and were thus better able to block UV. This is due to the fact that nano-particles have a larger surface area per unit mass and volume than the conventional materials, leading to the increase of the effectiveness of blocking UV radiation. For small particles, light scattering predominates at approximately one-tenth of the wavelength of the scattered light. Rayleigh's scattering theory stated that the scattering was strongly dependent upon the wavelength, where the scattering was inversely proportional to the wavelength to the fourth power. This theory predicts that in order to scatter UV radiation between 200 and 400 nm, the optimum particle size will be between 20 and

40 nm. UV-blocking treatment for cotton fabrics was developed using the sol-gel method. A thin layer of titanium dioxide is formed on the surface of the treated cotton fabric which provides excellent UV-protection; the effect can be maintained after 50 home launderings. Apart from water droplet rolls titanium dioxide, zinc oxide nano-rods of 10 to 50 nm in length were applied to cotton fabric to provide UV protection.

Flame Retardant Finish

Nyacol nano technologies, Inc., has been the world's leading supplier of colloidal antimony pentoxide which is used for flame retardant finish in textile. It offers colloidal antimony pentoxide us fine particle dispersion for use as a flame retardant synergist with halogenated flame-retardants. (The ratio of halogen to antimony is 5:1 to 2:1). Nano antimony pentoxide is used with Halogenated flame-retardants for a flame retardant finishes. 10 parts of nycal in 1550 parts of aqueous dispersion, with pH 7 and add 40 parts of H_2O and sufficient ammonia add for bring out pH 9, mix this with 50 parts of rubber latex and spray to the Non-woven material.

Wrinkle Resistance

To impart wrinkle resistance to fabric, resin is commonly used in conventional methods. However, there are limitations to applying resin, including a decrease in the tensile strength of fibre, abrasion resistance, water absorbency and dyeability, as well as breathability. To overcome the limitations of using resin, some researchers employed nano-titanium dioxide and nano-silica to improve the wrinkle resistance of cotton and silk respectively. Nano-titanium dioxide was employed with carboxylic acid as a catalyst under UV irradiation to catalyse the cross-linking reaction between the cellulose molecule and the acid. On the other hand, nano-silica was applied with maleic anhydride as a catalyst; the results showed that the application of nano-silica with maleic anhydride could successfully improve the wrinkle resistance of silk.

Nano Particles in Finishing

Nano particles such as metal oxides and ceramics are also used in textile finishing altering surface properties and imparting textile functions. Nano size particles have a larger surface area and hence higher efficiency than larger size particles. Besides, nanosize particles are transparent, and do not blur colour and brightness of the textile substrates. However, preventing nano particles from aggregation is the key to achieve a desired performance. As an example, the fabric treated with nano particles TiCh and MgO replaces fabrics with active carbon, previously used as chemical and biological protective materials. The photocatalytic activity of TiO_2 and MgO nano particles can break harmful and toxic chemicals and biological agents. These nano particles can be pre-engineered to adhere to textile substrates by using spray coating or electrostatic methods. Finishing with nano particles can convert fabrics into sensor-based materials. If nano-crystalline piezo ceramic particles are incorporated into fabrics, the finished fabric can convert exerted mechanical forces into electrical signals enabling the monitoring of bodily functions such as heart rhythm and pulse if they are worn next to sky Next Generation Carefree Finishing that withstands 50 Washes.

Nano-Care

The nano-care finished fabric is shown in Figure 10.1. It is a technology that brings about an entirely carefree fabric with wrinkle resistant, shrink proof, water and stain repellent properties, intended for use in cellulosic fibres such as cotton and linen. It is a next-generation, ease-of-care, dimension-stabilizing finish, one step ahead of methods that simply give wrinkle resistance and shrink-proofing. Nano-Care withstands more than 50 home launderings. It imparts water repellency and stain resistance superior to those of conventional methods, maintaining high water and oil repellency levels (80 and 4) even after 20 home washes.

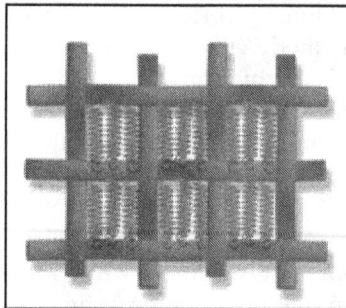

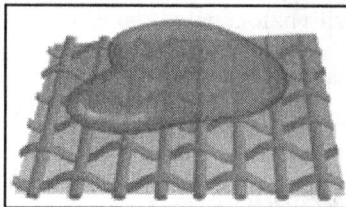

Figure 10.1: Nano-care Finishing of Fabric.

Key Features

☆ Superior Stain, Water, and Oil Repellency

☆ Resists Wrinkles

☆ Breathable Fabric

☆ Preserves Original Hand

☆ Easy Care

Nano-Pel

This nanotech application of water-and-oil repellent finishing is effective for use in natural fibres such as cotton, linen, wool and silk, as well as synthetics such as polyester, nylon and acryl. Unsurpassed performance in durability and water and oil repellency may be expected particularly with natural fibres. Nano-Pel cotton withstands 50 home launderings, with functionality levels well-maintained for water and oil repellency (80 and 4) even after 20 washes.

Key Features

☆ Superior Water and Oil Repellency

☆ Minimize Stains

☆ Breathable Fabric

☆ Preserves Original Hand

☆ Easy Care

☆ Durable Performance

Nano-Dry

It is a hydrophilic finishing technology that imparts outstanding endurance of more than 50 home launderings and offers prospects of considerable contribution to the area of polyester and nylon synthetic garments. Nano-Dry exerts durability superior to that of the hydrophilic finishing of polyester commonly carried out in Japan using polyethylene glycol polymer molecules, and allows no dye migration when deep-dyed. It is expected to serve particularly well for use in nylon, as there exists no such durable hydrophilic finishing, in the field of sportswear and underwear that require perspiration absorbency. Considerable growth is expected within the forthcoming period of 3 to 6 months, mainly in the field of sportswear.

Key Features

☆ Moisture Wicking

☆ Retains Breathability of Fabric

☆ Quick Drying

☆ Preserves Original Hand

☆ Durable Performance

Nano-Touch

This ultimate finishing technology gives durable cellulose wrapping over synthetic fibre. Cellulosic sheath and synthetic core together form a concentric structure to bring overall solutions to the disadvantages of synthetics being hydrophobic, electrostatic, having artificial hand and glaring luster. It will broaden the existing use of synthetics, being free of their disadvantages as found in synthetic suits being hydrophobic, electrostatic and having unnatural hand. The following are examples of new areas of use created through Nano-Touch, a new standard for fibre compounding. Self-assembled nano-layer (SAN) coating is a challenge to traditional textile coating. Research in this area is still in embryo stage. In self-assembled nano-layer (SAN) coating, target chemical molecules form a layer of thickness less than nanometer on the surface of textile materials. Additional layers can be added on the top of the existing ones creating a nano-layered structure. Different SAN approaches are being explored to confer special functions to textile materials.

Key Features

☆ Superior Refinement in a Blended Fabric

☆ Durable Performance

☆ Luxurious Cotton-Like Hand

☆ Easy Care

☆ Reduced Static Build-up

The self-assembly process begins by exposing a charged surface to a solution of an oppositely charged polyelectrolyte. The amount of adsorbed material is self-limiting by the charge density of the substrate. Surplus polymer solution adhering to the support is removed by simply washing it in a neutral solution. Under the proper conditions, the polyion is adsorbed with more than the stoichiometric number of charges relative to the substrate, reversing the sign of the surface charge. In consequence, when the substrate is exposed to a second solution containing a polyion of opposite charge, an additional polyion layer is adsorbed reversing in this way the sign of the surface charge once again. Consecutive cycles with alternating adsorption of poly-anions and poly-cations result in step-wise growth in total thickness of polymer films.

Index

A

Accessories 84
Acid donors 38
Acid dyes 35
Acid milling dyes 36
Acidifying 20
Adequate number 24
Adjustable squeezing devices 22
Adsorbable organic halogens (AOX) 3
Air brush 93
Airflow 65
Alcoholysis 47
Alkali cellulose 19
Alkaline 3
Ammonia mercerizing 3, 26
Ancillary operations 71
Animal forms 83
Anti-static finish 98
Antimicrobial finishes 97
AOX 32

Aromatic amines 41, 47
Auxiliaries 15
Azoic colourants 47

B

Bandhani 94
Basic (cationic) dyes 38
Basins 84
Batch orocesses 62
Batik 88, 89
Bio-eliminability 41, 43, 54
Black colour solution 81
Bleaching 3, 29
Bleaching treatment 3
Block printed 79
Block printing 81, 90
Brushes 88
Bundling 85
Burning behaviour 7

C

Carboximethyl cellulose (CMC) 13

Carriers 41

Causticizing 27

Caustification 3

Cellulose derivates 13

Cellulose fibres 26

Chain mercerizing machine 20

Chainless cloth mercerising ranges 22

Chainless system 25

Chemical characteristics 42

Chlorine dioxide gas 32

Choking 9

COD 14

Colour paste preparation 67

Combustion 8

Complexing agents 51

Continuous processes 65

Conventional prints 79

Cotton 1, 7

Crackled design 89

Cutting 82

D

De-foaming agents 14

Defoamers 38

Desizing 2, 13

Developing 81

Digital printing 78

Direct style 4

Discharge printing 69, 94

Discharging agents 68

Discontinuous processes 17

Dispersants 40

Disperse dyes 40

Dispersing agents 39, 51

Disulphonated 36

Drafting 20

DTPA 30

Dye 84

Dye calculation 87

Dye proportion 90

Dyeing 4, 57

Dyes 35, 37, 68

Dyestuffs 1

E

Eco-toxicity 40

EDTA 30

Effluent contamination 41

Electrolytes 39, 43

Environmental issues 38, 41

F

Fabric 89

Fabric entrance 22

Fabric entrance section 20

Fabric in rope form 62

Fabric speed 9

Fabrics 88

Fat 2, 14

Fibre 37

Fibre elasticity 26

Finishing 97

Fixation 67, 70

Flame burner 9

Flame intensity 8

Flame retardant finish 99

Flame width 9

Flat-screen printing 71

Flax 1

Flock 1

G

Galactomannans 13

Gas singeing machine 7

Gluconates 30

Gun spray 93

H

Hand painted 79
Hank dyeing machines 59
Heavy metals 44
Horizontal spindle machines 59
Human forms 84
Hydrogen peroxide 4, 29
Hydrolysis 49
Hydrophilic characteristics 1

I

Ikkat fabrics 95
Impregnation section 20
Ink-jet printing 78
Inorganic substances 3

J

Jet dyeing machine 63
Jet printing 75

K

Kalamkari 79, 80
Knitted fabrics 1
Knotting 84

L

Large wooden spoons 84
Leuco-sulphur dyes 51
Levelling agents 43
Liquid ammonia mercersing process 26
Loose fibre 5, 57
Low shrinkage post washing 26
Lye impregnation 22

M

Madhubani wall painting 82
Marbling 85
Mercerising effect 24
Mercerization 19
Mercerizing 3
Metal-complex Dyes 41

Molecular weight fragments 7
Mono sulphonated 36
Mordant dyes (chrome dyes) 43
Multi-colour Design 89
Myrobelums 80

N

Nano particles in finishing 99
Nano-care 100
Nano-dry 100
Nano-pel 100
Nano-touch 101
NaOH 15, 38
Naphthol dyes 46, 86
Neutralizing 24
NH_3 salts 38
NTA 30

O

Objects resist tying 85
Odour fights finish 98
Organic halogens 41, 43, 50
Overflow 64
Oxidation 52

P

Package dyeing machines 59
Padding 20
Painting 82
Paste preparation 68
Patola 95
Pectin 2
Peracetic acid 32
pH regulators 38, 43
Phosphonates 30
Pigments 35, 68
Plate singeing machine 6
Pleating 85
Polyacrylates 14, 30
Polyamide 42

Polyester 7, 14
Polyvinyl acetate 14
Polyvinyl alcohols (PVA) 14
Precautions 87
Preservatives 14
Pretreatment processes 1
Printed textile 84
Printing 4, 67
Protein derivates 13
Proteins 3
Protruding fibre 5

R

Rapid colours 90
Reactive dyes 47
Recuperation 24
Reducing agents 41
Resist style 4
Rinsing 20
Roller printing 75, 93
Rotary cylinder singeing machine 6
Rotary-screen printing 74

S

Salt 49
Scouring 2
Screen printing 91
Silk 1
Singed fabrics 5
Singeing 2, 5
Sodium chlorite 3, 4, 29, 32
Sodium hypochlorite 4, 29
Soft-flow 65
Solubilising agents 38
Spider web 85
Sponges 93
Stabilization 24
Stabilizing section 20
Starch 13

Starch-based sizes 15
Steam recuperation zone 20
Steaming 91
Stencil printing 92
Stencil sheets 92
Strongly polar 1:2 complexes 43
Sulphur dyes 50
Sulphuric acid 91
Super milling dyes 36
Symbols 83

T

TAK printing system 78
Tensile strength 26
Tension regulation system 25
Thickeners 41
Thickening agents 38
Tie 84
Tied portion 88
Tiny dots 85
Tjanting 88
Tjap 88
Toxicology 41
Tritic 85
Tube type machines 61

U

Unfixed colourants 41, 47
Urea 49
UV-protection 98

V

Vat dyes 52, 86
Vatting 52
Versatility 25
Vertical spindle machines 61
Viscosity regulators 14

W

Washing 20, 81
Washing Zone 25

Water soluble sizes 15
Water soluble sulphur dyes 51
Water soluble synthetic size 1
Wax 88, 89
Waxes 2
Weakly polar 1:2 complexes 43
Wetting 39
Wetting agents 14
White thread 84
Width stretching 20

Winch beck 62
Wool 1
Woven 1, 3
Wrinkle resistance 26

X
X-ray pattern 19

Y
Yarn 1, 59
Yarns 5
Yellow colour 81

www.ingramcontent.com/pod-product-compliance
Lightning Source LLC
Chambersburg PA
CBHW050229270326
41914CB00003BA/640